Virginia Communication and Literacy

Assessment

SECRETS

Study Guide
Your Key to Exam Success

VCLA Test Review for the Virginia Communication and Literacy Assessment

Dear Future Exam Success Story:

First of all, **THANK YOU** for purchasing Mometrix study materials!

Second, congratulations! You are one of the few determined test-takers who are committed to doing whatever it takes to excel on your exam. **You have come to the right place.** We developed these study materials with one goal in mind: to deliver you the information you need in a format that's concise and easy to use.

In addition to optimizing your guide for the content of the test, we've outlined our recommended steps for breaking down the preparation process into small, attainable goals so you can make sure you stay on track.

We've also analyzed the entire test-taking process, identifying the most common pitfalls and showing how you can overcome them and be ready for any curveball the test throws you.

Standardized testing is one of the biggest obstacles on your road to success, which only increases the importance of doing well in the high-pressure, high-stakes environment of test day. Your results on this test could have a significant impact on your future, and this guide provides the information and practical advice to help you achieve your full potential on test day.

Your success is our success

We would love to hear from you! If you would like to share the story of your exam success or if you have any questions or comments in regard to our products, please contact us at **800-673-8175** or **support@mometrix.com**.

Thanks again for your business and we wish you continued success!

Sincerely,
The Mometrix Test Preparation Team

Need more help? Check out our flashcards at: http://MometrixFlashcards.com/VIRGINIA

TABLE OF CONTENTS

Introduction

Thank you for purchasing this resource! You have made the choice to prepare yourself for a test that could have a huge impact on your future, and this guide is designed to help you be fully ready for test day. Obviously, it's important to have a solid understanding of the test material, but you also need to be prepared for the unique environment and stressors of the test, so that you can perform to the best of your abilities.

For this purpose, the first section that appears in this guide is the **Secret Keys**. We've devoted countless hours to meticulously researching what works and what doesn't, and we've boiled down our findings to the five most impactful steps you can take to improve your performance on the test. We start at the beginning with study planning and move through the preparation process, all the way to the testing strategies that will help you get the most out of what you know when you're finally sitting in front of the test.

We recommend that you start preparing for your test as far in advance as possible. However, if you've bought this guide as a last-minute study resource and only have a few days before your test, we recommend that you skip over the first two Secret Keys since they address a long-term study plan.

If you struggle with **test anxiety**, we strongly encourage you to check out our recommendations for how you can overcome it. Test anxiety is a formidable foe, but it can be beaten, and we want to make sure you have the tools you need to defeat it.

Secret Key #1 – Plan Big, Study Small

There's a lot riding on your performance. If you want to ace this test, you're going to need to keep your skills sharp and the material fresh in your mind. You need a plan that lets you review everything you need to know while still fitting in your schedule. We'll break this strategy down into three categories.

Information Organization

Start with the information you already have: the official test outline. From this, you can make a complete list of all the concepts you need to cover before the test. Organize these concepts into groups that can be studied together, and create a list of any related vocabulary you need to learn so you can brush up on any difficult terms. You'll want to keep this vocabulary list handy once you actually start studying since you may need to add to it along the way.

Time Management

Once you have your set of study concepts, decide how to spread them out over the time you have left before the test. Break your study plan into small, clear goals so you have a manageable task for each day and know exactly what you're doing. Then just focus on one small step at a time. When you manage your time this way, you don't need to spend hours at a time studying. Studying a small block of content for a short period each day helps you retain information better and avoid stressing over how much you have left to do. You can relax knowing that you have a plan to cover everything in time. In order for this strategy to be effective though, you have to start studying early and stick to your schedule. Avoid the exhaustion and futility that comes from last-minute cramming!

Study Environment

The environment you study in has a big impact on your learning. Studying in a coffee shop, while probably more enjoyable, is not likely to be as fruitful as studying in a quiet room. It's important to keep distractions to a minimum. You're only planning to study for a short block of time, so make the most of it. Don't pause to check your phone or get up to find a snack. It's also important to **avoid multitasking**. Research has consistently shown that multitasking will make your studying dramatically less effective. Your study area should also be comfortable and well-lit so you don't have the distraction of straining your eyes or sitting on an uncomfortable chair.

The time of day you study is also important. You want to be rested and alert. Don't wait until just before bedtime. Study when you'll be most likely to comprehend and remember. Even better, if you know what time of day your test will be, set that time aside for study. That way your brain will be used to working on that subject at that specific time and you'll have a better chance of recalling information.

Finally, it can be helpful to team up with others who are studying for the same test. Your actual studying should be done in as isolated an environment as possible, but the work of organizing the information and setting up the study plan can be divided up. In between study sessions, you can discuss with your teammates the concepts that you're all studying and quiz each other on the details. Just be sure that your teammates are as serious about the test as you are. If you find that your study time is being replaced with social time, you might need to find a new team.

Secret Key #2 – Make Your Studying Count

You're devoting a lot of time and effort to preparing for this test, so you want to be absolutely certain it will pay off. This means doing more than just reading the content and hoping you can remember it on test day. It's important to make every minute of study count. There are two main areas you can focus on to make your studying count:

Retention

It doesn't matter how much time you study if you can't remember the material. You need to make sure you are retaining the concepts. To check your retention of the information you're learning, try recalling it at later times with minimal prompting. Try carrying around flashcards and glance at one or two from time to time or ask a friend who's also studying for the test to quiz you.

To enhance your retention, look for ways to put the information into practice so that you can apply it rather than simply recalling it. If you're using the information in practical ways, it will be much easier to remember. Similarly, it helps to solidify a concept in your mind if you're not only reading it to yourself but also explaining it to someone else. Ask a friend to let you teach them about a concept you're a little shaky on (or speak aloud to an imaginary audience if necessary). As you try to summarize, define, give examples, and answer your friend's questions, you'll understand the concepts better and they will stay with you longer. Finally, step back for a big picture view and ask yourself how each piece of information fits with the whole subject. When you link the different concepts together and see them working together as a whole, it's easier to remember the individual components.

Finally, practice showing your work on any multi-step problems, even if you're just studying. Writing out each step you take to solve a problem will help solidify the process in your mind, and you'll be more likely to remember it during the test.

Modality

Modality simply refers to the means or method by which you study. Choosing a study modality that fits your own individual learning style is crucial. No two people learn best in exactly the same way, so it's important to know your strengths and use them to your advantage.

For example, if you learn best by visualization, focus on visualizing a concept in your mind and draw an image or a diagram. Try color-coding your notes, illustrating them, or creating symbols that will trigger your mind to recall a learned concept. If you learn best by hearing or discussing information, find a study partner who learns the same way or read aloud to yourself. Think about how to put the information in your own words. Imagine that you are giving a lecture on the topic and record yourself so you can listen to it later.

For any learning style, flashcards can be helpful. Organize the information so you can take advantage of spare moments to review. Underline key words or phrases. Use different colors for different categories. Mnemonic devices (such as creating a short list in which every item starts with the same letter) can also help with retention. Find what works best for you and use it to store the information in your mind most effectively and easily.

Secret Key #3 – Practice the Right Way

Your success on test day depends not only on how many hours you put into preparing, but also on whether you prepared the right way. It's good to check along the way to see if your studying is paying off. One of the most effective ways to do this is by taking practice tests to evaluate your progress. Practice tests are useful because they show exactly where you need to improve. Every time you take a practice test, pay special attention to these three groups of questions:

- The questions you got wrong
- The questions you had to guess on, even if you guessed right
- The questions you found difficult or slow to work through

This will show you exactly what your weak areas are, and where you need to devote more study time. Ask yourself why each of these questions gave you trouble. Was it because you didn't understand the material? Was it because you didn't remember the vocabulary? Do you need more repetitions on this type of question to build speed and confidence? Dig into those questions and figure out how you can strengthen your weak areas as you go back to review the material.

Additionally, many practice tests have a section explaining the answer choices. It can be tempting to read the explanation and think that you now have a good understanding of the concept. However, an explanation likely only covers part of the question's broader context. Even if the explanation makes sense, **go back and investigate** every concept related to the question until you're positive you have a thorough understanding.

As you go along, keep in mind that the practice test is just that: practice. Memorizing these questions and answers will not be very helpful on the actual test because it is unlikely to have any of the same exact questions. If you only know the right answers to the sample questions, you won't be prepared for the real thing. **Study the concepts** until you understand them fully, and then you'll be able to answer any question that shows up on the test.

It's important to wait on the practice tests until you're ready. If you take a test on your first day of study, you may be overwhelmed by the amount of material covered and how much you need to learn. Work up to it gradually.

On test day, you'll need to be prepared for answering questions, managing your time, and using the test-taking strategies you've learned. It's a lot to balance, like a mental marathon that will have a big impact on your future. Like training for a marathon, you'll need to start slowly and work your way up. When test day arrives, you'll be ready.

Start with the strategies you've read in the first two Secret Keys—plan your course and study in the way that works best for you. If you have time, consider using multiple study resources to get different approaches to the same concepts. It can be helpful to see difficult concepts from more than one angle. Then find a good source for practice tests. Many times, the test website will suggest potential study resources or provide sample tests.

Practice Test Strategy

If you're able to find at least three practice tests, we recommend this strategy:

Untimed and Open-Book Practice

Take the first test with no time constraints and with your notes and study guide handy. Take your time and focus on applying the strategies you've learned.

Timed and Open-Book Practice

Take the second practice test open-book as well, but set a timer and practice pacing yourself to finish in time.

Timed and Closed-Book Practice

Take any other practice tests as if it were test day. Set a timer and put away your study materials. Sit at a table or desk in a quiet room, imagine yourself at the testing center, and answer questions as quickly and accurately as possible.

Keep repeating timed and closed-book tests on a regular basis until you run out of practice tests or it's time for the actual test. Your mind will be ready for the schedule and stress of test day, and you'll be able to focus on recalling the material you've learned.

Secret Key #4 – Pace Yourself

Once you're fully prepared for the material on the test, your biggest challenge on test day will be managing your time. Just knowing that the clock is ticking can make you panic even if you have plenty of time left. Work on pacing yourself so you can build confidence against the time constraints of the exam. Pacing is a difficult skill to master, especially in a high-pressure environment, so **practice is vital**.

Set time expectations for your pace based on how much time is available. For example, if a section has 60 questions and the time limit is 30 minutes, you know you have to average 30 seconds or less per question in order to answer them all. Although 30 seconds is the hard limit, set 25 seconds per question as your goal, so you reserve extra time to spend on harder questions. When you budget extra time for the harder questions, you no longer have any reason to stress when those questions take longer to answer.

Don't let this time expectation distract you from working through the test at a calm, steady pace, but keep it in mind so you don't spend too much time on any one question. Recognize that taking extra time on one question you don't understand may keep you from answering two that you do understand later in the test. If your time limit for a question is up and you're still not sure of the answer, mark it and move on, and come back to it later if the time and the test format allow. If the testing format doesn't allow you to return to earlier questions, just make an educated guess; then put it out of your mind and move on.

On the easier questions, be careful not to rush. It may seem wise to hurry through them so you have more time for the challenging ones, but it's not worth missing one if you know the concept and just didn't take the time to read the question fully. Work efficiently but make sure you understand the question and have looked at all of the answer choices, since more than one may seem right at first.

Even if you're paying attention to the time, you may find yourself a little behind at some point. You should speed up to get back on track, but do so wisely. Don't panic; just take a few seconds less on each question until you're caught up. Don't guess without thinking, but do look through the answer choices and eliminate any you know are wrong. If you can get down to two choices, it is often worthwhile to guess from those. Once you've chosen an answer, move on and don't dwell on any that you skipped or had to hurry through. If a question was taking too long, chances are it was one of the harder ones, so you weren't as likely to get it right anyway.

On the other hand, if you find yourself getting ahead of schedule, it may be beneficial to slow down a little. The more quickly you work, the more likely you are to make a careless mistake that will affect your score. You've budgeted time for each question, so don't be afraid to spend that time. Practice an efficient but careful pace to get the most out of the time you have.

Secret Key #5 – Have a Plan for Guessing

When you're taking the test, you may find yourself stuck on a question. Some of the answer choices seem better than others, but you don't see the one answer choice that is obviously correct. What do you do?

The scenario described above is very common, yet most test takers have not effectively prepared for it. Developing and practicing a plan for guessing may be one of the single most effective uses of your time as you get ready for the exam.

In developing your plan for guessing, there are three questions to address:

- When should you start the guessing process?
- How should you narrow down the choices?
- Which answer should you choose?

When to Start the Guessing Process

Unless your plan for guessing is to select C every time (which, despite its merits, is not what we recommend), you need to leave yourself enough time to apply your answer elimination strategies. Since you have a limited amount of time for each question, that means that if you're going to give yourself the best shot at guessing correctly, you have to decide quickly whether or not you will guess.

Of course, the best-case scenario is that you don't have to guess at all, so first, see if you can answer the question based on your knowledge of the subject and basic reasoning skills. Focus on the key words in the question and try to jog your memory of related topics. Give yourself a chance to bring the knowledge to mind, but once you realize that you don't have (or you can't access) the knowledge you need to answer the question, it's time to start the guessing process.

It's almost always better to start the guessing process too early than too late. It only takes a few seconds to remember something and answer the question from knowledge. Carefully eliminating wrong answer choices takes longer. Plus, going through the process of eliminating answer choices can actually help jog your memory.

Summary: Start the guessing process as soon as you decide that you can't answer the question based on your knowledge.

How to Narrow Down the Choices

The next chapter in this book (**Test-Taking Strategies**) includes a wide range of strategies for how to approach questions and how to look for answer choices to eliminate. You will definitely want to read those carefully, practice them, and figure out which ones work best for you. Here though, we're going to address a mindset rather than a particular strategy.

Your chances of guessing an answer correctly depend on how many options you are choosing from.

How many choices you have	How likely you are to guess correctly
5	20%
4	25%
3	33%
2	50%
1	100%

You can see from this chart just how valuable it is to be able to eliminate incorrect answers and make an educated guess, but there are two things that many test takers do that cause them to miss out on the benefits of guessing:

- Accidentally eliminating the correct answer
- Selecting an answer based on an impression

We'll look at the first one here, and the second one in the next section.

To avoid accidentally eliminating the correct answer, we recommend a thought exercise called **the $5 challenge**. In this challenge, you only eliminate an answer choice from contention if you are willing to bet $5 on it being wrong. Why $5? Five dollars is a small but not insignificant amount of money. It's an amount you could afford to lose but wouldn't want to throw away. And while losing $5 once might not hurt too much, doing it twenty times will set you back $100. In the same way, each small decision you make—eliminating a choice here, guessing on a question there—won't by itself impact your score very much, but when you put them all together, they can make a big difference. By holding each answer choice elimination decision to a higher standard, you can reduce the risk of accidentally eliminating the correct answer.

The $5 challenge can also be applied in a positive sense: If you are willing to bet $5 that an answer choice *is* correct, go ahead and mark it as correct.

Summary: Only eliminate an answer choice if you are willing to bet $5 that it is wrong.

Which Answer to Choose

You're taking the test. You've run into a hard question and decided you'll have to guess. You've eliminated all the answer choices you're willing to bet $5 on. Now you have to pick an answer. Why do we even need to talk about this? Why can't you just pick whichever one you feel like when the time comes?

The answer to these questions is that if you don't come into the test with a plan, you'll rely on your impression to select an answer choice, and if you do that, you risk falling into a trap. The test writers know that everyone who takes their test will be guessing on some of the questions, so they intentionally write wrong answer choices to seem plausible. You still have to pick an answer though, and if the wrong answer choices are designed to look right, how can you ever be sure that you're not falling for their trap? The best solution we've found to this dilemma is to take the decision out of your hands entirely. Here is the process we recommend:

Once you've eliminated any choices that you are confident (willing to bet $5) are wrong, select the first remaining choice as your answer.

Whether you choose to select the first remaining choice, the second, or the last, the important thing is that you use some preselected standard. Using this approach guarantees that you will not be enticed into selecting an answer choice that looks right, because you are not basing your decision on how the answer choices look.

This is not meant to make you question your knowledge. Instead, it is to help you recognize the difference between your knowledge and your impressions. There's a huge difference between thinking an answer is right because of what you know, and thinking an answer is right because it looks or sounds like it should be right.

Summary: To ensure that your selection is appropriately random, make a predetermined selection from among all answer choices you have not eliminated.

Test-Taking Strategies

This section contains a list of test-taking strategies that you may find helpful as you work through the test. By taking what you know and applying logical thought, you can maximize your chances of answering any question correctly!

It is very important to realize that every question is different and every person is different: no single strategy will work on every question, and no single strategy will work for every person. That's why we've included all of them here, so you can try them out and determine which ones work best for different types of questions and which ones work best for you.

Question Strategies

Read Carefully

Read the question and answer choices carefully. Don't miss the question because you misread the terms. You have plenty of time to read each question thoroughly and make sure you understand what is being asked. Yet a happy medium must be attained, so don't waste too much time. You must read carefully, but efficiently.

Contextual Clues

Look for contextual clues. If the question includes a word you are not familiar with, look at the immediate context for some indication of what the word might mean. Contextual clues can often give you all the information you need to decipher the meaning of an unfamiliar word. Even if you can't determine the meaning, you may be able to narrow down the possibilities enough to make a solid guess at the answer to the question.

Prefixes

If you're having trouble with a word in the question or answer choices, try dissecting it. Take advantage of every clue that the word might include. Prefixes and suffixes can be a huge help. Usually they allow you to determine a basic meaning. Pre- means before, post- means after, pro - is positive, de- is negative. From prefixes and suffixes, you can get an idea of the general meaning of the word and try to put it into context.

Hedge Words

Watch out for critical hedge words, such as *likely, may, can, sometimes, often, almost, mostly, usually, generally, rarely,* and *sometimes.* Question writers insert these hedge phrases to cover every possibility. Often an answer choice will be wrong simply because it leaves no room for exception. Be on guard for answer choices that have definitive words such as *exactly* and *always.*

Switchback Words

Stay alert for *switchbacks.* These are the words and phrases frequently used to alert you to shifts in thought. The most common switchback words are *but, although,* and *however.* Others include *nevertheless, on the other hand, even though, while, in spite of, despite, regardless of.* Switchback words are important to catch because they can change the direction of the question or an answer choice.

Face Value

When in doubt, use common sense. Accept the situation in the problem at face value. Don't read too much into it. These problems will not require you to make wild assumptions. If you have to go beyond creativity and warp time or space in order to have an answer choice fit the question, then you should move on and consider the other answer choices. These are normal problems rooted in reality. The applicable relationship or explanation may not be readily apparent, but it is there for you to figure out. Use your common sense to interpret anything that isn't clear.

Answer Choice Strategies

Answer Selection

The most thorough way to pick an answer choice is to identify and eliminate wrong answers until only one is left, then confirm it is the correct answer. Sometimes an answer choice may immediately seem right, but be careful. The test writers will usually put more than one reasonable answer choice on each question, so take a second to read all of them and make sure that the other choices are not equally obvious. As long as you have time left, it is better to read every answer choice than to pick the first one that looks right without checking the others.

Answer Choice Families

An answer choice family consists of two (in rare cases, three) answer choices that are very similar in construction and cannot all be true at the same time. If you see two answer choices that are direct opposites or parallels, one of them is usually the correct answer. For instance, if one answer choice says that quantity x increases and another either says that quantity x decreases (opposite) or says that quantity y increases (parallel), then those answer choices would fall into the same family. An answer choice that doesn't match the construction of the answer choice family is more likely to be incorrect. Most questions will not have answer choice families, but when they do appear, you should be prepared to recognize them.

Eliminate Answers

Eliminate answer choices as soon as you realize they are wrong, but make sure you consider all possibilities. If you are eliminating answer choices and realize that the last one you are left with is also wrong, don't panic. Start over and consider each choice again. There may be something you missed the first time that you will realize on the second pass.

Avoid Fact Traps

Don't be distracted by an answer choice that is factually true but doesn't answer the question. You are looking for the choice that answers the question. Stay focused on what the question is asking for so you don't accidentally pick an answer that is true but incorrect. Always go back to the question and make sure the answer choice you've selected actually answers the question and is not merely a true statement.

Extreme Statements

In general, you should avoid answers that put forth extreme actions as standard practice or proclaim controversial ideas as established fact. An answer choice that states the "process should be used in certain situations, if..." is much more likely to be correct than one that states the "process should be discontinued completely." The first is a calm rational statement and doesn't even make a definitive, uncompromising stance, using a hedge word *if* to provide wiggle room, whereas the second choice is a radical idea and far more extreme.

Benchmark

As you read through the answer choices and you come across one that seems to answer the question well, mentally select that answer choice. This is not your final answer, but it's the one that will help you evaluate the other answer choices. The one that you selected is your benchmark or standard for judging each of the other answer choices. Every other answer choice must be compared to your benchmark. That choice is correct until proven otherwise by another answer choice beating it. If you find a better answer, then that one becomes your new benchmark. Once you've decided that no other choice answers the question as well as your benchmark, you have your final answer.

Predict the Answer

Before you even start looking at the answer choices, it is often best to try to predict the answer. When you come up with the answer on your own, it is easier to avoid distractions and traps because you will know exactly what to look for. The right answer choice is unlikely to be word-for-word what you came up with, but it should be a close match. Even if you are confident that you have the right answer, you should still take the time to read each option before moving on.

General Strategies

Tough Questions

If you are stumped on a problem or it appears too hard or too difficult, don't waste time. Move on! Remember though, if you can quickly check for obviously incorrect answer choices, your chances of guessing correctly are greatly improved. Before you completely give up, at least try to knock out a couple of possible answers. Eliminate what you can and then guess at the remaining answer choices before moving on.

Check Your Work

Since you will probably not know every term listed and the answer to every question, it is important that you get credit for the ones that you do know. Don't miss any questions through careless mistakes. If at all possible, try to take a second to look back over your answer selection and make sure you've selected the correct answer choice and haven't made a costly careless mistake (such as marking an answer choice that you didn't mean to mark). This quick double check should more than pay for itself in caught mistakes for the time it costs.

Pace Yourself

It's easy to be overwhelmed when you're looking at a page full of questions; your mind is confused and full of random thoughts, and the clock is ticking down faster than you would like. Calm down and maintain the pace that you have set for yourself. Especially as you get down to the last few minutes of the test, don't let the small numbers on the clock make you panic. As long as you are on track by monitoring your pace, you are guaranteed to have time for each question.

Don't Rush

It is very easy to make errors when you are in a hurry. Maintaining a fast pace in answering questions is pointless if it makes you miss questions that you would have gotten right otherwise. Test writers like to include distracting information and wrong answers that seem right. Taking a little extra time to avoid careless mistakes can make all the difference in your test score. Find a pace that allows you to be confident in the answers that you select.

Keep Moving

Panicking will not help you pass the test, so do your best to stay calm and keep moving. Taking deep breaths and going through the answer elimination steps you practiced can help to break through a stress barrier and keep your pace.

Final Notes

The combination of a solid foundation of content knowledge and the confidence that comes from practicing your plan for applying that knowledge is the key to maximizing your performance on test day. As your foundation of content knowledge is built up and strengthened, you'll find that the strategies included in this chapter become more and more effective in helping you quickly sift through the distractions and traps of the test to isolate the correct answer.

Now it's time to move on to the test content chapters of this book, but be sure to keep your goal in mind. As you read, think about how you will be able to apply this information on the test. If you've already seen sample questions for the test and you have an idea of the question format and style, try to come up with questions of your own that you can answer based on what you're reading. This will give you valuable practice applying your knowledge in the same ways you can expect to on test day.

Good luck and good studying!

Reading

Understanding Literature

Reading literature is a different experience than reading non-fiction works. Our imagination is more active as we review what we have read, imagine ourselves as characters in the novel, and try to guess what will happen next. Suspense, surprise, fantasy, fear, anxiety, compassion, and a host of other emotions and feelings may be stirred by a provocative novel.

Reading longer works of fiction is a cumulative process. Some elements of a novel have a great impact, while others may go virtually unnoticed. Therefore, as novels are read with a critical eye to language, it is helpful to perceive and identify larger patterns and movements in the work as a whole. This will benefit the reader by placing characters and events in perspective, and will enrich the reading experience greatly. Novels should be savored rather than gulped. Careful reading and thoughtful analysis of the major themes of the novel are essential to a clear understanding of the work.

One of the most important skills in reading comprehension is the identification of **topics** and **main ideas.** There is a subtle difference between these two features. The topic is the subject of a text, or what the text is about. The main idea, on the other hand, is the most important point being made by the author. The topic is usually expressed in a few words at the most, while the main idea often needs a full sentence to be completely defined. As an example, a short passage might have the topic of penguins and the main idea *Penguins are different from other birds in many ways.* In most nonfiction writing, the topic and the main idea will be stated directly, often in a sentence at the very beginning or end of the text. When being tested on an understanding of the author's topic, the reader can quickly *skim* the passage for the general idea, stopping to read only the first sentence of each paragraph. A paragraph's first sentence is often (but not always) the main topic sentence, and it gives you a summary of the content of the paragraph. However, there are cases in which the reader must figure out an unstated topic or main idea. In these instances, the student must read every sentence of the text, and try to come up with an overarching idea that is supported by each of those sentences.

> **Review Video:** Topics and Main Ideas
> Visit mometrix.com/academy and enter code: 407801

While the main idea is the overall premise of a story, **supporting details** provide evidence and backing for the main point. In order to show that a main idea is correct, or valid, the author needs to add details that prove their point. All texts contain details, but they are only classified as supporting details when they serve to reinforce some larger point. Supporting details are most commonly found in informative and persuasive texts. In some cases, they will be clearly indicated with words like *for example* or *for instance*, or they will be enumerated with words like *first*, *second*, and *last*. However, they may not be indicated with special words. As a reader, it is important to consider whether the author's supporting details really back up his or her main point. Supporting details can be factual and correct but still not relevant to the author's point. Conversely, supporting details can seem pertinent but be ineffective because they are based on opinion or assertions that cannot be proven.

> **Review Video:** Supporting Details
> Visit mometrix.com/academy and enter code: 396297

An example of a main idea is: "Giraffes live in the Serengeti of Africa." A supporting detail about giraffes could be: "A giraffe uses its long neck to reach twigs and leaves on trees." The main idea gives the general idea that the text is about giraffes. The supporting detail gives a specific fact about how the giraffes eat.

As opposed to a main idea, themes are seldom expressed directly in a text, so they can be difficult to identify. A **theme** is an issue, an idea, or a question raised by the text. For instance, a theme of William Shakespeare's *Hamlet* is indecision, as the title character explores his own psyche and the results of his failure to make bold choices. A great work of literature may have many themes, and the reader is justified in identifying any for which he or she can find support. One common characteristic of themes is that they raise more questions than they answer. In a good piece of fiction, the author is not always trying to convince the reader, but is instead trying to elevate the reader's perspective and encourage him to consider the themes more deeply. When reading, one can identify themes by constantly asking what general issues the text is addressing. A good way to evaluate an author's approach to a theme is to begin reading with a question in mind (for example, how does this text approach the theme of love?) and then look for evidence in the text that addresses that question.

> **Review Video: Theme**
> Visit mometrix.com/academy and enter code: 732074

Purposes for Writing

In order to be an effective reader, one must pay attention to the author's **position** and purpose. Even those texts that seem objective and impartial, like textbooks, have some sort of position and bias. Readers need to take these positions into account when considering the author's message. When an author uses emotional language or clearly favors one side of an argument, his position is clear. However, the author's position may be evident not only in what he writes, but in what he doesn't write. For this reason, it is sometimes necessary to review some other texts on the same topic in order to develop a view of the author's position. If this is not possible, then it may be useful to acquire a little background personal information about the author. When the only source of information is the text, however, the reader should look for language and argumentation that seems to indicate a particular stance on the subject.

> **Review Video: Author's Position**
> Visit mometrix.com/academy and enter code: 827954

Identifying the **purpose** of an author is usually easier than identifying her position. In most cases, the author has no interest in hiding his or her purpose. A text that is meant to entertain, for instance, should be obviously written to please the reader. Most narratives, or stories, are written to entertain, though they may also inform or persuade. Informative texts are easy to identify as well. The most difficult purpose of a text to identify is persuasion, because the author has an interest in making this purpose hard to detect. When a person knows that the author is trying to convince him, he is automatically more wary and skeptical of the argument. For this reason persuasive texts often try to establish an entertaining tone, hoping to amuse the reader into agreement, or an informative tone, hoping to create an appearance of authority and objectivity.

An author's purpose is often evident in the organization of the text. For instance, if the text has headings and subheadings, if key terms are in bold, and if the author makes his main idea clear from the beginning, then the likely purpose of the text is to inform. If the author begins by making a claim and then makes various arguments to support that claim, the purpose is probably to persuade. If the author is telling a story, or is more interested in holding the attention of the reader than in making a particular point or delivering information, then his purpose is most likely to entertain. As a reader, it is best to judge an author on how well he accomplishes his purpose. In other words, it is not entirely fair to complain that a textbook is boring: if the text is clear and easy to understand, then the author has done his job. Similarly, a storyteller should not be judged too harshly for getting some facts wrong, so long as he is able to give pleasure to the reader.

> **Review Video: Purpose of an Author**
> Visit mometrix.com/academy and enter code: 497555

The author's purpose for writing will affect his writing style and the response of the reader. In a **persuasive essay**, the author is attempting to change the reader's mind or convince him of something he did not believe previously. There are several identifying characteristics of persuasive writing. One is opinion presented as fact. When an author attempts to persuade the reader, he often presents his or her opinions as if they were fact. A reader must be on guard for statements that sound factual but which cannot be subjected to research, observation, or experiment. Another characteristic of persuasive writing is emotional language. An author will often try to play on the reader's emotion by appealing to his sympathy or sense of morality. When an author uses colorful or evocative language with the intent of arousing the reader's passions, it is likely that he is attempting to persuade. Finally, in many cases a persuasive text will give an unfair explanation of opposing positions, if these positions are mentioned at all.

An **informative text** is written to educate and enlighten the reader. Informative texts are almost always nonfiction, and are rarely structured as a story. The intention of an informative text is to deliver information in the most comprehensible way possible, so the structure of the text is likely to be very clear. In an informative text, the thesis statement is often in the first sentence. The author may use some colorful language, but is likely to put more emphasis on clarity and precision. Informative essays do not typically appeal to the emotions. They often contain facts and figures, and rarely include the opinion of the author. Sometimes a persuasive essay can resemble an informative essay, especially if the author maintains an even tone and presents his or her views as if they were established fact.

The success or failure of an author's intent to **entertain** is determined by those who read the author's work. Entertaining texts may be either fiction or nonfiction, and they may describe real or imagined people, places, and events. Entertaining texts are often narratives, or stories. A text that is written to entertain is likely to contain colorful language that engages the imagination and the emotions. Such writing often features a great deal of figurative language, which typically enlivens its subject matter with images and analogies. Though an entertaining text is not usually written to persuade or inform, it may accomplish both of these tasks. An entertaining text may appeal to the reader's emotions and cause him or her to think differently about a particular subject. In any case, entertaining texts tend to showcase the personality of the author more so than do other types of writing.

When an author intends to **express feelings,** she may use colorful and evocative language. An author may write emotionally for any number of reasons. Sometimes, the author will do so because she is describing a personal situation of great pain or happiness. Sometimes an author is attempting to persuade the reader, and so will use emotion to stir up the passions. It can be easy to identify this kind of expression when the writer uses phrases like *I felt* and *I sense*. However, sometimes the author will simply describe feelings without introducing them. As a reader, it is important to recognize when an author is expressing emotion, and not to become overwhelmed by sympathy or passion. A reader should maintain some detachment so that he or she can still evaluate the strength of the author's argument or the quality of the writing.

In a sense, almost all writing is descriptive, insofar as it seeks to describe events, ideas, or people to the reader. Some texts, however, are primarily concerned with **description**. A descriptive text focuses on a particular subject, and attempts to depict it in a way that will be clear to the reader. Descriptive texts contain many adjectives and adverbs, words that give shades of meaning and create a more detailed mental picture for the reader. A descriptive text fails when it is unclear or vague to the reader. On the other hand, however, a descriptive text that compiles too much detail can be boring and overwhelming to the reader. A descriptive text will certainly be informative, and it may be persuasive and entertaining as well. Descriptive writing is a challenge for the author, but when it is done well, it can be fun to read.

Writing Devices

Authors will use different stylistic and writing devices to make their meaning more clearly understood. One of those devices is comparison and contrast. When an author describes the ways in which two things are alike, he or she is **comparing** them. When the author describes the ways in which two things are different, he or she is **contrasting** them. The "compare and contrast" essay is one of the most common forms in nonfiction. It is often signaled with certain words: a comparison may be indicated with such words as *both, same, like, too,* and *as well*; while a contrast may be indicated by words like *but, however, on the other hand, instead,* and *yet*. Of course, comparisons and contrasts may be implicit without using any such signaling language. A single sentence may both compare and contrast. Consider the sentence *Brian and Sheila love ice cream, but Brian prefers vanilla and Sheila prefers strawberry*. In one sentence, the author has described both a similarity (love of ice cream) and a difference (favorite flavor).

> **Review Video:** <u>Compare and Contrast</u>
> Visit mometrix.com/academy and enter code: 798319

One of the most common text structures is **cause and effect**. A cause is an act or event that makes something happen, and an effect is the thing that happens as a result of that cause. A cause-and-effect relationship is not always explicit, but there are some words in English that signal causality, such as *since, because,* and *as a result*. As an example, consider the sentence *Because the sky was clear, Ron did not bring an umbrella*. The cause is the clear sky, and the effect is that Ron did not bring an umbrella. However, sometimes the cause-and-effect relationship will not be clearly noted. For instance, the sentence *He was late and missed the meeting* does not contain any signaling words, but it still contains a cause (he was late) and an effect (he missed the meeting). It is possible for a single cause to have multiple effects, or for a single effect to have multiple causes. Also, an effect can in turn be the cause of another effect, in what is known as a cause-and-effect chain.

Authors often use analogies to add meaning to the text. An **analogy** is a comparison of two things. The words in the analogy are connected by a certain, often undetermined relationship. Look at this analogy: moo is to cow as quack is to duck. This analogy compares the sound that a cow makes with the sound that a duck makes. Even if the word 'quack' was not given, one could figure out it is the correct word to complete the analogy based on the relationship between the words 'moo' and 'cow'. Some common relationships for analogies include synonyms, antonyms, part to whole, definition, and actor to action.

Another element that impacts a text is the author's point of view. The **point of view** of a text is the perspective from which it is told. The author will always have a point of view about a story before he draws up a plot line. The author will know what events they want to take place, how they want the characters to interact, and how the story will resolve. An author will also have an opinion on the topic, or series of events, which is presented in the story, based on their own prior experience and beliefs.

The two main points of view that authors use are first person and third person. If the narrator of the story is also the main character, or *protagonist*, the text is written in first-person point of view. In first person, the author writes with the word *I*. Third-person point of view is probably the most common point of view that authors use. Using third person, authors refer to each character using the words *he* or *she*. In third-person omniscient, the narrator is not a character in the story and tells the story of all of the characters at the same time.

> **Review Video: Point of View**
> Visit mometrix.com/academy and enter code: 383336

A good writer will use **transitional words** and phrases to guide the reader through the text. You are no doubt familiar with the common transitions, though you may never have considered how they operate. Some transitional phrases (*after, before, during, in the middle of*) give information about time. Some indicate that an example is about to be given (*for example, in fact, for instance*). Writers use them to compare (*also, likewise*) and contrast (*however, but, yet*). Transitional words and phrases can suggest addition (*and, also, furthermore, moreover*) and logical relationships (*if, then, therefore, as a result, since*). Finally, transitional words and phrases can demarcate the steps in a process (*first, second, last*). You should incorporate transitional words and phrases where they will orient your reader and illuminate the structure of your composition.

> **Review Video: Transitional Words and Phrases**
> Visit mometrix.com/academy and enter code: 197796

Types of Passages

A **narrative** passage is a story. Narratives can be fiction or nonfiction. However, there are a few elements that a text must have in order to be classified as a narrative. To begin with, the text must have a plot. That is, it must describe a series of events. If it is a good narrative, these events will be interesting and emotionally engaging to the reader. A narrative also has characters. These could be people, animals, or even inanimate objects, so long as they participate in the plot. A narrative passage often contains figurative language, which is meant to stimulate the imagination of the reader by making comparisons and observations. A metaphor, which is a description of one thing in terms of another, is a common piece of figurative language. *The moon was a frosty snowball* is an example of a metaphor: it is obviously untrue in the literal sense, but it suggests a certain mood for the reader. Narratives often proceed in a clear sequence, but they do not need to do so.

An **expository** passage aims to inform and enlighten the reader. It is nonfiction and usually centers around a simple, easily defined topic. Since the goal of exposition is to teach, such a passage should be as clear as possible. It is common for an expository passage to contain helpful organizing words, like *first, next, for example*, and *therefore*. These words keep the reader oriented in the text. Although expository passages do not need to feature colorful language and artful writing, they are often more effective when they do. For a reader, the challenge of expository passages is to maintain steady attention. Expository passages are not always about subjects in which a reader will naturally be interested, and the writer is often more concerned with clarity and comprehensibility than with engaging the reader. For this reason, many expository passages are dull. Making notes is a good way to maintain focus when reading an expository passage.

A **technical** passage is written to describe a complex object or process. Technical writing is common in medical and technological fields, in which complicated mathematical, scientific, and engineering ideas need to be explained simply and clearly. To ease comprehension, a technical passage usually proceeds in a very logical order. Technical passages often have clear headings and subheadings, which are used to keep the reader oriented in the text. It is also common for these passages to break sections up with numbers or letters. Many technical passages look more like an outline than a piece of prose. The amount of jargon or difficult vocabulary will vary in a technical passage depending on the intended audience. As much as possible, technical passages try to avoid language that the reader will have to research in order to understand the message. Of course, it is not always possible to avoid jargon.

A **persuasive** passage is meant to change the reader's mind or lead her into agreement with the author. The persuasive intent may be obvious, or it may be quite difficult to discern. In some cases, a persuasive passage will be indistinguishable from an informative passage: it will make an assertion and offer supporting details. However, a persuasive passage is more likely to make claims based on opinion and to appeal to the reader's emotions. Persuasive passages may not describe alternate positions and, when they do, they often display significant bias. It may be clear that a persuasive passage is giving the author's viewpoint, or the passage may adopt a seemingly objective tone. A persuasive passage is successful if it can make a convincing argument and win the trust of the reader.

A persuasive essay will likely focus on one central argument, but it may make many smaller claims along the way. These are subordinate arguments with which the reader must agree if he or she is going to agree with the central argument. The central argument will only be as strong as the subordinate claims. These claims should be rooted in fact and observation, rather than subjective judgment. The best persuasive essays provide enough supporting detail to justify claims without overwhelming the reader. Remember that a fact must be susceptible to independent verification: that is, it must be something the reader could confirm. Also, statistics are only effective when they take into account possible objections. For instance, a statistic on the number of foreclosed houses would only be useful if it was taken over a defined interval and in a defined area. Most readers are wary of statistics, because they are so often misleading. If possible, a persuasive essay should always include references so that the reader can obtain more information. Of course, this means that the writer's accuracy and fairness may be judged by the inquiring reader.

Opinions are formed by emotion as well as reason, and persuasive writers often appeal to the feelings of the reader. Although readers should always be skeptical of this technique, it is often used in a proper and ethical manner. For instance, there are many subjects that have an obvious emotional component, and therefore cannot be completely treated without an appeal to the emotions. Consider an article on drunk driving: it makes sense to include some specific examples that will alarm or sadden the reader. After all, drunk driving often has serious and tragic consequences. Emotional appeals are not appropriate, however, when they attempt to mislead the reader. For instance, in political advertisements it is common to emphasize the patriotism of the preferred candidate, because this will encourage the audience to link their own positive feelings about the country with their opinion of the candidate. However, these ads often imply that the other candidate is unpatriotic, which in most cases is far from the truth. Another common and improper emotional appeal is the use of loaded language, as for instance referring to an avidly religious person as a "fanatic" or a passionate environmentalist as a "tree hugger." These terms introduce an emotional component that detracts from the argument.

History and Culture

Historical context has a profound influence on literature: the events, knowledge base, and assumptions of an author's time color every aspect of his or her work. Sometimes, authors hold opinions and use language that would be considered inappropriate or immoral in a modern setting, but that was acceptable in the author's time. As a reader, one should consider how the historical context influenced a work and also how today's opinions and ideas shape the way modern readers read the works of the past. For instance, in most societies of the past, women were treated as second-class citizens. An author who wrote in 18th-century England might sound sexist to modern readers, even if that author was relatively feminist in his time. Readers should not have to excuse the faulty assumptions and prejudices of the past, but they should appreciate that a person's thoughts and words are, in part, a result of the time and culture in which they live or lived, and it is perhaps unfair to expect writers to avoid all of the errors of their times.

Even a brief study of world literature suggests that writers from vastly different cultures address similar themes. For instance, works like the *Odyssey* and *Hamlet* both tackle the individual's battle for self-control and independence. In every culture, authors address themes of personal growth and the struggle for maturity. Another universal theme is the conflict between the individual and society. In works as culturally disparate as *Native Son*, the *Aeneid*, and *1984*, authors dramatize how people struggle to maintain their personalities and dignity in large, sometimes oppressive groups. Finally, many cultures have versions of the hero's (or heroine's) journey, in which an adventurous person must overcome many obstacles in order to gain greater knowledge, power, and perspective. Some famous works that treat this theme are the *Epic of Gilgamesh*, Dante's *Divine Comedy*, and *Don Quixote*.

Authors from different genres (for instance poetry, drama, novel, short story) and cultures may address similar themes, but they often do so quite differently. For instance, poets are likely to address subject matter obliquely, through the use of images and allusions. In a play, on the other hand, the author is more likely to dramatize themes by using characters to express opposing viewpoints. This disparity is known as a dialectical approach. In a novel, the author does not need to express themes directly; rather, they can be illustrated through events and actions. In some regional literatures, like those of Greece or England, authors use more irony: their works have characters that express views and make decisions that are clearly disapproved of by the author. In Latin America, there is a great tradition of using supernatural events to illustrate themes about real life. In China and Japan, authors frequently use well-established regional forms (haiku, for instance) to organize their treatment of universal themes.

Responding to Literature

When reading good literature, the reader is moved to engage actively in the text. One part of being an active reader involves making predictions. A **prediction** is a guess about what will happen next. Readers are constantly making predictions based on what they have read and what they already know. Consider the following sentence: *Staring at the computer screen in shock, Kim blindly reached over for the brimming glass of water on the shelf to her side.* The sentence suggests that Kim is agitated and that she is not looking at the glass she is going to pick up, so a reader might predict that she is going to knock the glass over. Of course, not every prediction will be accurate: perhaps Kim will pick the glass up cleanly. Nevertheless, the author has certainly created the expectation that the water might be spilled. Predictions are always subject to revision as the reader acquires more information.

> **Review Video: Predictions**
> Visit mometrix.com/academy and enter code: 437248

Test-taking tip: To respond to questions requiring future predictions, the student's answers should be based on evidence of past or present behavior.

Readers are often required to understand text that claims and suggests ideas without stating them directly. An **inference** is a piece of information that is implied but not written outright by the author. For instance, consider the following sentence: *Mark made more money that week than he had in the previous year*. From this sentence, the reader can infer that Mark either has not made much money in the previous year or made a great deal of money that week. Often, a reader can use information he or she already knows to make inferences. Take as an example the sentence *When his coffee arrived, he looked around the table for the silver cup*. Many people know that cream is typically served in a silver cup, so using their own base of knowledge they can infer that the subject of this sentence takes his coffee with cream. Making inferences requires concentration, attention, and practice.

> **Review Video: Inference**
> Visit mometrix.com/academy and enter code: 379203

Test-taking tip: While being tested on his ability to make correct inferences, the student must look for contextual clues. An answer can be *true* but not *correct*. The contextual clues will help you find the answer that is the best answer out of the given choices. Understand the context in which a phrase is stated. When asked for the implied meaning of a statement made in the passage, the student should immediately locate the statement and read the context in which it was made. Also, look for an answer choice that has a similar phrase to the statement in question.

A reader must be able to identify a text's **sequence**, or the order in which things happen. Often, and especially when the sequence is very important to the author, it is indicated with signal words like *first*, *then*, *next*, and *last*. However, sometimes a sequence is merely implied and must be noted by the reader. Consider the sentence *He walked in the front door and switched on the hall lamp*. Clearly, the man did not turn the lamp on before he walked in the door, so the implied sequence is that he first walked in the door and then turned on the lamp. Texts do not always proceed in an orderly sequence from first to last: sometimes, they begin at the end and then start over at the beginning. As a reader, it can be useful to make brief notes to clarify the sequence.

In addition to inferring and predicting things about the text, the reader must often **draw conclusions** about the information he has read. When asked for a *conclusion* that may be drawn, look for critical "hedge" phrases, such as *likely*, *may*, *can*, *will often*, among many others. When you are being tested on this knowledge, remember that question writers insert these hedge phrases to cover every possibility. Often an answer will be wrong simply because it leaves no room for exception. Extreme positive or negative answers (such as always, never, etc.) are usually not correct. The reader should not use any outside knowledge that is not gathered from the reading passage to answer the related questions. Correct answers can be derived straight from the reading passage.

Literary Genres

Literary genres refer to the basic generic types of poetry, drama, fiction, and nonfiction. Literary genre is a method of classifying and analyzing literature. There are numerous subdivisions within genre, including such categories as novels, novellas, and short stories in fiction. Drama may also be subdivided into comedy, tragedy, and many other categories. Poetry and nonfiction have their own distinct divisions.

Genres often overlap, and the distinctions among them are blurred, such as that between the nonfiction novel and docudrama, as well as many others. However, the use of genres is helpful to the reader as a set of understandings that guide our responses to a work. The generic norm sets expectations and forms the framework within which we read and evaluate a work. This framework will guide both our understanding and interpretation of the work. It is a useful tool for both literary criticism and analysis.

Fiction is a general term for any form of literary narrative that is invented or imagined rather than being factual. For those individuals who equate fact with truth, the imagined or invented character of fiction tends to render it relatively unimportant or trivial among the genres. Defenders of fiction are quick to point out that the fictional mode is an essential part of being. The ability to imagine or discuss what-if plots, characters, and events is clearly part of the human experience.

Prose is derived from the Latin and means "straightforward discourse." Prose fiction, although having many categories, may be divided into three main groups:

- **Short stories**: a fictional narrative, the length of which varies, usually under 20,000 words. Short stories usually have only a few characters and generally describe one major event or insight. The short story began in magazines in the late 1800s and has flourished ever since.
- **Novels**: a longer work of fiction, often containing a large cast of characters and extensive plotting. The emphasis may be on an event, action, social problems, or any experience. There is now a genre of nonfiction novels pioneered by Truman Capote's *In Cold Blood* in the 1960s. Novels may also be written in verse.
- **Novellas**: a work of narrative fiction longer than a short story but shorter than a novel. Novellas may also be called short novels or novelettes. They originated from the German tradition and have become common forms in all of the world's literature.

Many elements influence a work of prose fiction. Some important ones are:

- **Speech and dialogue**: Characters may speak for themselves or through the narrator. Dialogue may be realistic or fantastic, depending on the author's aim.
- **Thoughts and mental processes**: There may be internal dialogue used as a device for plot development or character understanding.
- **Dramatic involvement**: Some narrators encourage readers to become involved in the events of the story, whereas others attempt to distance readers through literary devices.
- **Action**: This is any information that advances the plot or involves new interactions between the characters.
- **Duration**: The time frame of the work may be long or short, and the relationship between described time and narrative time may vary.
- **Setting and description**: Is the setting critical to the plot or characters? How are the action scenes described?
- **Themes**: This is any point of view or topic given sustained attention.
- **Symbolism**: Authors often veil meanings through imagery and other literary constructions.

- 23 -

Fiction is much wider than simply prose fiction. Songs, ballads, epics, and narrative poems are examples of non-prose fiction. A full definition of fiction must include not only the work itself but also the framework in which it is read. Literary fiction can also be defined as not true rather than nonexistent, as many works of historical fiction refer to real people, places, and events that are treated imaginatively as if they were true. These imaginary elements enrich and broaden literary expression.

When analyzing fiction, it is important for the reader to look carefully at the work being studied. The plot or action of a narrative can become so entertaining that the language of the work is ignored. The language of fiction should not simply be a way to relate a plot—it should also yield many insights to the judicious reader. Some prose fiction is based on the reader's engagement with the language rather than the story. A studious reader will analyze the mode of expression as well as the narrative. Part of the reward of reading in this manner is to discover how the author uses different language to describe familiar objects, events, or emotions. Some works focus the reader on an author's unorthodox use of language, whereas others may emphasize characters or storylines. What happens in a story is not always the critical element in the work. This type of reading may be difficult at first but yields great rewards.

The **narrator** is a central part of any work of fiction, and can give insight about the purpose of the work and its main themes and ideas. The following are important questions to address to better understand the voice and role of the narrator and incorporate that voice into an overall understanding of the novel:

- Who is the narrator of the novel? What is the narrator's perspective, first person or third person? What is the role of the narrator in the plot? Are there changes in narrators or the perspective of narrators?
- Does the narrator explain things in the novel, or does meaning emerge from the plot and events? The personality of the narrator is important. She may have a vested interest in a character or event described. Some narratives follow the time sequence of the plot, whereas others do not. A narrator may express approval or disapproval about a character or events in the work.
- Tone is an important aspect of the narration. Who is actually being addressed by the narrator? Is the tone familiar or formal, intimate or impersonal? Does the vocabulary suggest clues about the narrator?

A **character** is a person intimately involved with the plot and development of the novel. Development of the novel's characters not only moves the story along but will also tell the reader a lot about the novel itself. There is usually a physical description of the character, but this is often omitted in modern and postmodern novels. These works may focus on the psychological state or motivation of the character. The choice of a character's name may give valuable clues to his role in the work.

Characters are said to be flat or round. Flat characters tend to be minor figures in the story, changing little or not at all. Round characters (those understood from a well-rounded view) are more central to the story and tend to change as the plot unfolds. Stock characters are similar to flat characters, filling out the story without influencing it.

Modern literature has been greatly affected by Freudian psychology, giving rise to such devices as the interior monologue and magical realism as methods of understanding characters in a work. These give the reader a more complex understanding of the inner lives of the characters and enrich the understanding of relationships between characters.

> **Review Video: Characters**
> Visit mometrix.com/academy and enter code: 429493

Another important genre is that of **drama**: a play written to be spoken aloud. The drama is in many ways inseparable from performance. Reading drama ideally involves using imagination to visualize and re-create the play with characters and settings. The reader stages the play in his imagination, watching characters interact and developments unfold. Sometimes this involves simulating a theatrical presentation; other times it involves imagining the events. In either case, the reader is imagining the unwritten to re-create the dramatic experience. Novels present some of the same problems, but a narrator will provide much more information about the setting, characters, inner dialogues, and many other supporting details. In drama, much of this is missing, and we are required to use our powers of projection and imagination to taste the full flavor of the dramatic work. There are many empty spaces in dramatic texts that must be filled by the reader to fully appreciate the work.

> **Review Video: Dramas**
> Visit mometrix.com/academy and enter code: 216060

When reading drama in this way, there are some advantages over watching the play performed (though there is much criticism in this regard):

- Freedom of point of view and perspective: Text is free of interpretations of actors, directors, producers, and technical staging.
- Additional information: The text of a drama may be accompanied by notes or prefaces placing the work in a social or historical context. Stage directions may also provide relevant information about the author's purpose. None of this is typically available at live or filmed performances.
- Study and understanding: Difficult or obscure passages may be studied at leisure and supplemented by explanatory works. This is particularly true of older plays with unfamiliar language, which cannot be fully understood without an opportunity to study the material.

Critical elements of drama, especially when it is being read aloud or performed, include dialect, speech, and dialogue. Analysis of speech and dialogue is important in the critical study of drama. Some playwrights use speech to develop their characters. Speeches may be long or short, and written in as normal prose or blank verse. Some characters have a unique way of speaking which illuminates aspects of the drama. Emphasis and tone are both important, as well. Does the author make clear the tone in which lines are to be spoken, or is this open to interpretation? Sometimes there are various possibilities in tone with regard to delivering lines.

Dialect is any distinct variety of a language, especially one spoken in a region or part of a country. The criterion for distinguishing dialects from languages is that of mutual understanding. For example, people who speak Dutch cannot understand English unless they have learned it. But a speaker from Amsterdam can understand one from Antwerp; therefore, they speak different dialects of the same language. This is, however, a matter of degree; there are languages in which different dialects are unintelligible.

Dialect mixtures are the presence in one form of speech with elements from different neighboring dialects. The study of speech differences from one geographical area to another is called dialect geography. A dialect atlas is a map showing distribution of dialects in a given area. A dialect continuum shows a progressive shift in dialects across a territory, such that adjacent dialects are understandable, but those at the extremes are not.

Dramatic dialogue can be difficult to interpret and changes depending upon the tone used and which words are emphasized. Where the stresses, or meters, of dramatic dialogue fall can determine meaning. Variations in emphasis are only one factor in the manipulability of dramatic speech. Tone is of equal or greater importance and expresses a range of possible emotions and feelings that cannot be readily discerned from the script of a play. The reader must add tone to the words to understand the full meaning of a passage. Recognizing tone is a cumulative process as the reader begins to understand the characters and situations in the play. Other elements that influence the interpretation of dialogue include the setting, possible reactions of the characters to the speech, and possible gestures or facial expressions of the actor. There are no firm rules to guide the interpretation of dramatic speech. An open and flexible attitude is essential in interpreting dramatic dialogue.

Action is a crucial element in the production of a dramatic work. Many dramas contain little dialogue and much action. In these cases, it is essential for the reader to carefully study stage directions and visualize the action on the stage. Benefits of understanding stage directions include knowing which characters are on the stage at all times, who is speaking to whom, and following these patterns through changes of scene.

Stage directions also provide additional information, some of which is not available to a live audience. The nature of the physical space where the action occurs is vital, and stage directions help with this. The historical context of the period is important in understanding what the playwright was working with in terms of theaters and physical space. The type of staging possible for the author is a good guide to the spatial elements of a production.

Asides and soliloquies are devices that authors use in plot and character development. **Asides** indicate that not all characters are privy to the lines. This may be a method of advancing or explaining the plot in a subtle manner. **Soliloquies** are opportunities for character development, plot enhancement, and to give insight to characters' motives, feelings, and emotions. Careful study of these elements provides a reader with an abundance of clues to the major themes and plot of the work.

Art, music, and literature all interact in ways that contain many opportunities for the enrichment of all of the arts. Students could apply their knowledge of art and music by creating illustrations for a work or creating a musical score for a text. Students could discuss the meanings of texts and decide on their illustrations, or a score could amplify the meaning of the text.

Understanding the art and music of a period can make the experience of literature a richer, more rewarding experience. Students should be encouraged to use the knowledge of art and music to illuminate the text. Examining examples of dress, architecture, music, and dance of a period may be helpful in a fuller engagement of the text. Much of period literature lends itself to the analysis of the prevailing taste in art and music of an era, which helps place the literary work in a more meaningful context.

Opinions, Facts, and Fallacies

Critical thinking skills are mastered through understanding various types of writing and the different purposes that authors have for writing the way they do. Every author writes for a purpose. Understanding that purpose, and how they accomplish their goal, will allow you to critique the writing and determine whether or not you agree with their conclusions.

Readers must always be conscious of the distinction between fact and opinion. A **fact** can be subjected to analysis and can be either proved or disproved. An **opinion**, on the other hand, is the author's personal feeling, which may not be alterable by research, evidence, or argument. If the author writes that the distance from New York to Boston is about two hundred miles, he is stating a fact. But if he writes that New York is too crowded, then he is giving an opinion, because there is no objective standard for overpopulation. An opinion may be indicated by words like *believe*, *think*, or *feel*. Also, an opinion may be supported by facts: for instance, the author might give the population density of New York as a reason for why it is overcrowded. An opinion supported by fact tends to be more convincing. When authors support their opinions with other opinions, the reader is unlikely to be moved.

Facts should be presented to the reader from reliable sources. An opinion is what the author thinks about a given topic. An opinion is not common knowledge or proven by expert sources, but it is information that the author believes and wants the reader to consider. To distinguish between fact and opinion, a reader needs to look at the type of source that is presenting information, what information backs-up a claim, and whether or not the author may be motivated to have a certain point of view on a given topic. For example, if a panel of scientists has conducted multiple studies on the effectiveness of taking a certain vitamin, the results are more likely to be factual than if a company selling a vitamin claims that taking the vitamin can produce positive effects. The company is motivated to sell its product, while the scientists are using the scientific method to prove a theory. If the author uses words such as "I think...", the statement is an opinion.

> **Review Video: Fact or Opinion**
> Visit mometrix.com/academy and enter code: 870899

In their attempt to persuade, writers often make mistakes in their thinking patterns and writing choices. It's important to understand these so you can make an informed decision. Every author has a point of view, but when an author ignores reasonable counterarguments or distorts opposing viewpoints, she is demonstrating a **bias**. A bias is evident whenever the author is unfair or inaccurate in his or her presentation. Bias may be intentional or unintentional, but it should always alert the reader to be skeptical of the argument being made. It should be noted that a biased author may still be correct. However, the author will be correct in spite of her bias, not because of it. A **stereotype** is like a bias, except that it is specifically applied to a group or place. Stereotyping is considered to be particularly abhorrent because it promotes negative generalizations about people. Many people are familiar with some of the hateful stereotypes of certain ethnic, religious, and cultural groups. Readers should be very wary of authors who stereotype. These faulty assumptions typically reveal the author's ignorance and lack of curiosity.

> **Review Video: Bias and Stereotype**
> Visit mometrix.com/academy and enter code: 644829

Sometimes, authors will **appeal to the reader's emotion** in an attempt to persuade or to distract the reader from the weakness of the argument. For instance, the author may try to inspire the pity of the reader by delivering a heart-rending story. An author also might use the bandwagon approach, in which he suggests that his opinion is correct because it is held by the majority. Some authors resort to name-calling, in which insults and harsh words are delivered to the opponent in an attempt to distract. In advertising, a common appeal is the testimonial, in which a famous person endorses a product. Of course, the fact that a celebrity likes something should not really mean anything to the reader. These and other emotional appeals are usually evidence of poor reasoning and a weak argument.

> **Review Video: Appeal to Emotion**
> Visit mometrix.com/academy and enter code: 163442

Certain *logical fallacies* are frequent in writing. A logical fallacy is a failure of reasoning. As a reader, it is important to recognize logical fallacies, because they diminish the value of the author's message. The four most common logical fallacies in writing are the false analogy, circular reasoning, false dichotomy, and overgeneralization. In a **false analogy**, the author suggests that two things are similar, when in fact they are different. This fallacy is often committed when the author is attempting to convince the reader that something unknown is like something relatively familiar. The author takes advantage of the reader's ignorance to make this false comparison. One example might be the following statement: *Failing to tip a waitress is like stealing money out of somebody's wallet.* Of course, failing to tip is very rude, especially when the service has been good, but people are not arrested for failing to tip as they would for stealing money from a wallet. To compare stingy diners with thieves is a false analogy.

> **Review Video: False Analogy**
> Visit mometrix.com/academy and enter code: 865045

Circular reasoning is one of the more difficult logical fallacies to identify, because it is typically hidden behind dense language and complicated sentences. Reasoning is described as circular when it offers no support for assertions other than restating them in different words. Put another way, a circular argument refers to itself as evidence of truth. A simple example of circular argument is when a person uses a word to define itself, such as saying *Niceness is the state of being nice.* If the reader does not know what *nice* means, then this definition will not be very useful. In a text, circular reasoning is usually more complex. For instance, an author might say *Poverty is a problem for society because it creates trouble for people throughout the community.* It is redundant to say that poverty is a problem because it creates trouble. When an author engages in circular reasoning, it is often because he or she has not fully thought out the argument, or cannot come up with any legitimate justifications.

> **Review Video: Circular Reasoning**
> Visit mometrix.com/academy and enter code: 398925

One of the most common logical fallacies is the **false dichotomy**, in which the author creates an artificial sense that there are only two possible alternatives in a situation. This fallacy is common when the author has an agenda and wants to give the impression that his view is the only sensible one. A false dichotomy has the effect of limiting the reader's options and imagination. An example of a false dichotomy is the statement *You need to go to the party with me, otherwise you'll just be bored at home.* The speaker suggests that the only other possibility besides being at the party is being bored at home. But this is not true, as it is perfectly possible to be entertained at home, or even to go somewhere other than the party. Readers should always be wary of the false dichotomy: when an author limits alternatives, it is always wise to ask whether he is being valid.

Review Video: False Dichotomy
Visit mometrix.com/academy and enter code: 484397

Overgeneralization is a logical fallacy in which the author makes a claim that is so broad it cannot be proved or disproved. In most cases, overgeneralization occurs when the author wants to create an illusion of authority, or when he is using sensational language to sway the opinion of the reader. For instance, in the sentence *Everybody knows that she is a terrible teacher*, the author makes an assumption that cannot really be believed. This kind of statement is made when the author wants to create the illusion of consensus when none actually exists: it may be that most people have a negative view of the teacher, but to say that *everybody* feels that way is an exaggeration. When a reader spots overgeneralization, she should become skeptical about the argument that is being made, because an author will often try to hide a weak or unsupported assertion behind authoritative language.

Review Video: Overgeneralization
Visit mometrix.com/academy and enter code: 367357

Two other types of logical fallacies are **slippery slope** arguments and **hasty generalizations**. In a slippery slope argument, the author says that if something happens, it automatically means that something else will happen as a result, even though this may not be true. (i.e., just because you study hard does not mean you are going to ace the test). "Hasty generalization" is drawing a conclusion too early, without finishing analyzing the details of the argument. Writers of persuasive texts often use these techniques because they are very effective. In order to **identify logical fallacies**, readers need to read carefully and ask questions as they read. Thinking critically means not taking everything at face value. Readers need to critically evaluate an author's argument to make sure that the logic used is sound.

Organization of the Text

The way a text is organized can help the reader to understand more clearly the author's intent and his conclusions. There are various ways to organize a text, and each one has its own purposes and uses.

Some nonfiction texts are organized to **present a problem** followed by a solution. In this type of text, it is common for the problem to be explained before the solution is offered. In some cases, as when the problem is well known, the solution may be briefly introduced at the beginning. The entire passage may focus on the solution, and the problem will be referenced only occasionally. Some texts will outline multiple solutions to a problem, leaving the reader to choose among them. If the author has an interest or an allegiance to one solution, he may fail to mention or may describe inaccurately some of the other solutions. Readers should be careful of the author's agenda when reading a problem-solution text. Only by understanding the author's point of view and interests can one develop a proper judgment of the proposed solution.

Authors need to organize information logically so the reader can follow it and locate information within the text. Two common organizational structures are cause and effect and chronological order. When using **chronological order**, the author presents information in the order that it happened. For example, biographies are written in chronological order; the subject's birth and childhood are presented first, followed by their adult life, and lastly by the events leading up to the person's death.

In **cause and effect**, an author presents one thing that makes something else happen. For example, if one were to go to bed very late, they would be tired. The cause is going to bed late, with the effect of being tired the next day.

It can be tricky to identify the cause-and-effect relationships in a text, but there are a few ways to approach this task. To begin with, these relationships are often signaled with certain terms. When an author uses words like *because, since, in order*, and *so*, she is likely describing a cause-and-effect relationship. Consider the sentence, "He called her because he needed the homework." This is a simple causal relationship, in which the cause was his need for the homework and the effect was his phone call. Not all cause-and-effect relationships are marked in this way, however. Consider the sentences, "He called her. He needed the homework." When the cause-and-effect relationship is not indicated with a keyword, it can be discovered by asking why something happened. He called her: why? The answer is in the next sentence: He needed the homework.

Persuasive essays, in which an author tries to make a convincing argument and change the reader's mind, usually include cause-and-effect relationships. However, these relationships should not always be taken at face value. An author frequently will assume a cause or take an effect for granted. To read a persuasive essay effectively, one needs to judge the cause-and-effect relationships the author is presenting. For instance, imagine an author wrote the following: "The parking deck has been unprofitable because people would prefer to ride their bikes." The relationship is clear: the cause is that people prefer to ride their bikes, and the effect is that the parking deck has been unprofitable. However, a reader should consider whether this argument is conclusive. Perhaps there are other reasons for the failure of the parking deck: a down economy, excessive fees, etc. Too often, authors present causal relationships as if they are fact rather than opinion. Readers should be on the alert for these dubious claims.

Thinking critically about ideas and conclusions can seem like a daunting task. One way to make it easier is to understand the basic elements of ideas and writing techniques. Looking at the way different ideas relate to each other can be a good way for the reader to begin his analysis. For instance, sometimes writers will write about two different ideas that are in opposition to each other. The analysis of these opposing ideas is known as **contrast**. Contrast is often marred by the author's obvious partiality to one of the ideas. A discerning reader will be put off by an author who does not engage in a fair fight. In an analysis of opposing ideas, both ideas should be presented in their clearest and most reasonable terms. If the author does prefer a side, he should avoid indicating this preference with pejorative language. An analysis of opposing ideas should proceed through the major differences point by point, with a full explanation of each side's view. For instance, in an analysis of capitalism and communism, it would be important to outline each side's view on labor, markets, prices, personal responsibility, etc. It would be less effective to describe the theory of communism and then explain how capitalism has thrived in the West. An analysis of opposing views should present each side in the same manner.

Many texts follow the **compare-and-contrast** model, in which the similarities and differences between two ideas or things are explored. Analysis of the similarities between ideas is called comparison. In order for a comparison to work, the author must place the ideas or things in an equivalent structure. That is, the author must present the ideas in the same way. Imagine an author wanted to show the similarities between cricket and baseball. The correct way to do so would be to summarize the equipment and rules for each game. It would be incorrect to summarize the equipment of cricket and then lay out the history of baseball, since this would make it impossible for the reader to see the similarities. It is perhaps too obvious to say that an analysis of similar ideas should emphasize the similarities. Of course, the author should take care to include any differences that must be mentioned. Often, these small differences will only reinforce the more general similarity.

Drawing Conclusions

Authors should have a clear purpose in mind while writing. Especially when reading informational texts, it is important to understand the logical conclusion of the author's ideas. **Identifying this logical conclusion** can help the reader understand whether he agrees with the writer or not. Identifying a logical conclusion is much like making an inference: it requires the reader to combine the information given by the text with what he already knows to make a supportable assertion. If a passage is written well, then the conclusion should be obvious even when it is unstated. If the author intends the reader to draw a certain conclusion, then all of his argumentation and detail should be leading toward it. One way to approach the task of drawing conclusions is to make brief notes of all the points made by the author. When these are arranged on paper, they may clarify the logical conclusion. Another way to approach conclusions is to consider whether the reasoning of the author raises any pertinent questions. Sometimes it will be possible to draw several conclusions from a passage, and on occasion these will be conclusions that were never imagined by the author. It is essential, however, that these conclusions be supported directly by the text.

> **Review Video: Identifying Logical Conclusions**
> Visit mometrix.com/academy and enter code: 281653

The term **text evidence** refers to information that supports a main point or points in a story, and can help lead the reader to a conclusion. Information used as *text evidence* is precise, descriptive, and factual. A main point is often followed by supporting details that provide evidence to back-up a claim. For example, a story may include the claim that winter occurs during opposite months in the Northern and Southern hemispheres. *Text evidence* based on this claim may include countries where winter occurs in opposite months, along with reasons that winter occurs at different times of the year in separate hemispheres (due to the tilt of the Earth as it rotates around the sun).

Readers interpret text and respond to it in a number of ways. Using textual support helps defend your response or interpretation because it roots your thinking in the text. You are interpreting based on information in the text and not simply your own ideas. When crafting a response, look for important quotes and details from the text to help bolster your argument. If you are writing about a character's personality trait, for example, use details from the text to show that the character acted in such a way. You can also include statistics and facts from a nonfiction text to strengthen your response. For example, instead of writing, "A lot of people use cell phones," use statistics to provide the exact number. This strengthens your argument because it is more precise.

> **Review Video: Text Evidence**
> Visit mometrix.com/academy and enter code: 486236

The text used to support an argument can be the argument's downfall if it is not credible. A text is **credible**, or believable, when the author is knowledgeable and objective, or unbiased. The author's motivations for writing the text play a critical role in determining the credibility of the text and must be evaluated when assessing that credibility. The author's motives should be for the dissemination of information. The purpose of the text should be to inform or describe, not to persuade. When an author writes a persuasive text, he has the motivation that the reader will do what they want. The extent of the author's knowledge of the topic and their motivation must be evaluated when assessing the credibility of a text. Reports written about the Ozone layer by an environmental scientist and a hairdresser will have a different level of credibility.

After determining your own opinion and evaluating the credibility of your supporting text, it is sometimes necessary to communicate your ideas and findings to others. When **writing a response to a text**, it is important to use elements of the text to support your assertion or defend your position. Using supporting evidence from the text strengthens the argument because the reader can see how in depth the writer read the original piece and based their response on the details and facts within that text. Elements of text that can be used in a response include: facts, details, statistics, and direct quotations from the text. When writing a response, one must make sure they indicate which information comes from the original text and then base their discussion, argument, or defense around this information.

A reader should always be drawing conclusions from the text. Sometimes conclusions are implied from written information, and other times the information is **stated directly** within the passage. It is always more comfortable to draw conclusions from information stated within a passage, rather than to draw them from mere implications. At times an author may provide some information and then describe a counterargument. The reader should be alert for direct statements that are subsequently rejected or weakened by the author. The reader should always read the entire passage before drawing conclusions. Many readers are trained to expect the author's conclusions at either the beginning or the end of the passage, but many texts do not adhere to this format.

Drawing conclusions from information implied within a passage requires confidence on the part of the reader. **Implications** are things the author does not state directly, but which can be assumed based on what the author does say. For instance, consider the following simple passage: "I stepped outside and opened my umbrella. By the time I got to work, the cuffs of my pants were soaked." The author never states that it is raining, but this fact is clearly implied. Conclusions based on implication must be well supported by the text. In order to draw a solid conclusion, a reader should have multiple pieces of evidence, or, if he only has one, must be assured that there is no other possible explanation than his conclusion. A good reader will be able to draw many conclusions from information implied by the text, which enriches the reading experience considerably.

As an aid to drawing conclusions, the reader should be adept at **outlining** the information contained in the passage; an effective outline will reveal the structure of the passage, and will lead to solid conclusions. An effective outline will have a title that refers to the basic subject of the text, though it need not recapitulate the main idea. In most outlines, the main idea will be the first major section. It will have each major idea of the passage established as the head of a category. For instance, the most common outline format calls for the main ideas of the passage to be indicated with Roman numerals. In an effective outline of this kind, each of the main ideas will be represented by a Roman numeral and none of the Roman numerals will designate minor details or secondary ideas. Moreover, all supporting ideas and details should be placed in the appropriate place on the outline. An outline does not need to include every detail listed in the text, but it should feature all of those that are central to the argument or message. Each of these details should be listed under the appropriate main idea.

It is also helpful to **summarize** the information you have read in a paragraph or passage format. This process is similar to creating an effective outline. To begin with, a summary should accurately define the main idea of the passage, though it does not need to explain this main idea in exhaustive detail. It should continue by laying out the most important supporting details or arguments from the passage. All of the significant supporting details should be included, and none of the details included should be irrelevant or insignificant. Also, the summary should accurately report all of these details. Too often, the desire for brevity in a summary leads to the sacrifice of clarity or veracity. Summaries are often difficult to read, because they omit all of graceful language, digressions, and asides that distinguish great writing. However, if the summary is effective, it should contain much the same message as the original text.

Paraphrasing is another method the reader can use to aid in comprehension. When paraphrasing, one puts what they have read into their own words, rephrasing what the author has written to make it their own, to "translate" all of what the author says to their own words, including as many details as they can.

Informational Sources

Informational sources often come in short forms like a memo or recipe, or longer forms like books, magazines, or journals. These longer sources of information each have their own way of organizing information, but there are some similarities that the reader should be aware of.

Most books, magazines, and journals have a **table of contents** at the beginning. This helps the reader find the different parts of the book. The table of contents is usually found a page or two after the title page in a book, and on the first few pages of a magazine. However, many magazines now place the table of contents in the midst of an overabundance of advertisements, because they know readers will have to look at the ads as they search for the table. The standard orientation for a table of contents is the sections of the book listed along the left side, with the initial page number for each along the right. It is common in a book for the prefatory material (preface, introduction, etc.) to be numbered with Roman numerals. The contents are always listed in order from the beginning of the book to the end.

A nonfiction book will also typically have an **index** at the end so that the reader can easily find information about particular topics. An index lists the topics in alphabetical order. The names of people are listed with the last name first. For example, *Adams, John* would come before *Washington, George*. To the right of the entry, the relevant page numbers are listed. When a topic is mentioned over several pages, the index will often connect these pages with a dash. For instance, if the subject is mentioned from pages 35 to 42 and again on 53, then the index entry will be labeled as *35-42, 53*. Some entries will have subsets, which are listed below the main entry, indented slightly, and placed in alphabetical order. This is common for subjects that are discussed frequently in the book. For instance, in a book about Elizabethan drama, William Shakespeare will likely be an important topic. Beneath Shakespeare's name in the index, there might be listings for *death of*, *dramatic works of*, *life of*, etc. These more specific entries help the reader refine his search.

Many informative texts, especially textbooks, use **headings** and **subheadings** for organization. Headings and subheadings are typically printed in larger and bolder fonts, and are often in a different color than the main body of the text. Headings may be larger than subheadings. Also, headings and subheadings are not always complete sentences. A heading announces the topic that will be addressed in the text below. Headings are meant to alert the reader to what is about to come. Subheadings announce the topics of smaller sections within the entire section indicated by the heading. For instance, the heading of a section in a science textbook might be *AMPHIBIANS*, and within that section might be subheadings for *Frogs*, *Salamanders*, and *Newts*. Readers should always pay close attention to headings and subheadings, because they prime the brain for the information that is about to be delivered, and because they make it easy to go back and find particular details in a long text.

Reference Materials

Knowledge of reference materials such as dictionaries, encyclopedias, and manuals are vital for any reader. **Dictionaries** contain information about words. A standard dictionary entry begins with a pronunciation guide for the word. The entry will also give the word's part of speech: that is, whether it is a noun, verb, adjective, etc. A good dictionary will also include the word's origins, including the language from which it is derived and its meaning in that language. This information is known as the word's etymology.

Dictionary entries are in alphabetical order. Many words have more than one definition, in which case the definitions will be numbered. Also, if a word can be used as different parts of speech, its various definitions in those different capacities may be separated. A sample entry might look like this:

WELL: (adverb) 1. in a good way (noun) 1. a hole drilled into the earth

The correct definition of a word will vary depending on how it is used in a sentence. When looking up a word found while reading, the best way to determine the relevant definition is to substitute the dictionary's definitions for the word in the text, and select the definition that seems most appropriate.

Encyclopedias used to be the best source for general information on a range of common subjects. Many people took pride in owning a set of encyclopedias, which were often written by top researchers. Now, encyclopedias largely exist online. Although they no longer have a preeminent place in general scholarship, these digital encyclopedias now often feature audio and video clips. A good encyclopedia remains the best place to obtain basic information about a well-known topic. There are also specialty encyclopedias that cover more obscure or expert information. For instance, there are many medical encyclopedias that contain the detail and sophistication required by doctors. For a regular person researching a subject like ostriches, Pennsylvania, or the Crimean War, an encyclopedia is a good source.

A **thesaurus** is a reference book that gives synonyms of words. It is different from a dictionary because a thesaurus does not give definitions, only lists of synonyms. A thesaurus can be helpful in finding the meaning of an unfamiliar word when reading. If the meaning of a synonym is known, then the meaning of the unfamiliar word will be known. The other time a thesaurus is helpful is when writing. Using a thesaurus helps authors to vary their word choice.

A **database** is an informational source that has a different format than a publication or a memo. They are systems for storing and organizing large amounts of information. As personal computers have become more common and accessible, databases have become ever more present. The standard layout of a database is as a grid, with labels along the left side and the top. The horizontal rows and vertical columns that make up the grid are usually numbered or lettered, so that a particular square within the database might have a name like A3 or G5. Databases are good for storing information that can be expressed succinctly. They are most commonly used to store numerical data, but they also can be used to store the answers to yes-no questions and other brief data points. Information that is ambiguous (that is, has multiple possible meanings) or difficult to express in a few words is not appropriate for a database.

Often, a reader will come across a word that he does not recognize. The reader needs to know how to identify the definition of a word from its context. This means defining a word based on the words around it and the way it is used in a sentence. For instance, consider the following sentence: *The elderly scholar spent his evenings hunched over arcane texts that few other people even knew existed.*

The adjective *arcane* is uncommon, but the reader can obtain significant information about it based on its use here. Based on the fact that few other people know of their existence, the reader can assume that arcane texts must be rare and only of interest to a few people. And, because they are being read by an elderly scholar, the reader can assume that they focus on difficult academic subjects. Sometimes, words can even be defined by what they are not. For instance, consider the following sentence: *Ron's fealty to his parents was not shared by Karen, who disobeyed their every command.* Because someone who disobeys is not demonstrating *fealty*, the word can be inferred to mean something like obedience or respect.

When conducting research, it is important to depend on reputable **primary sources**. A primary source is the documentary evidence closest to the subject being studied. For instance, the primary sources for an essay about penguins would be photographs and recordings of the birds, as well as accounts of people who have studied penguins in person. A secondary source would be a review of a movie about penguins or a book outlining the observations made by others. A primary source should be credible and, if it is on a subject that is still being explored, recent. One way to assess the credibility of a work is to see how often it is mentioned in other books and articles on the same subject. Just by reading the works cited and bibliographies of other books, one can get a sense of what are the acknowledged authorities in the field.

The Internet was once considered a poor place to find sources for an essay or article, but its credibility has improved greatly over the years. Still, students need to exercise caution when performing research online. The best sources are those affiliated with established institutions, like universities, public libraries, and think tanks. Most newspapers are available online, and many of them allow the public to browse their archives. Magazines frequently offer similar services. When obtaining information from an unknown website, however, one must exercise considerably more caution. A website can be considered trustworthy if it is referenced by other sites that are known to be reputable. Also, credible sites tend to be properly maintained and frequently updated. A site is easier to trust when the author provides some information about him or herself, including some credentials that indicate expertise in the subject matter.

Organizing and Understanding Graphic Information

Two of the most common ways to organize ideas from a text, paraphrasing and summarizing, are verbal ways to organize data. Ideas from a text can also be organized using **graphic organizers**. A graphic organizer is a way to simplify information and just take key points from the text. A graphic organizer such as a timeline may have an event listed for a corresponding date on the timeline, whereas an outline may have an event listed under a key point that occurs in the text. Each reader needs to create the type of graphic organizer that works the best for him or her in terms of being able to recall information from a story. Examples include a *spider-map*, which takes a main idea from the story and places it in a bubble, with supporting points branching off the main idea, an *outline,* useful for diagramming the main and supporting points of the entire story, and a *Venn diagram,* which classifies information as separate or overlapping.

These graphic organizers can also be used by authors to enliven their presentation or text, but this may be counterproductive if the graphics are confusing or misleading. A graph should strip the author's message down to the essentials. It should have a clear title, and should be in the appropriate format. Authors may elect to use tables, line or bar graphs, or pie charts to illustrate their message. Each of these formats is correct for different types of data. The graphic should be large enough to read, and should be divided into appropriate categories. For instance, if the text is about the differences between federal spending on the military and on the space program, a pie chart or a bar graph would be the most effective choices. The pie chart could show each type of spending as a portion of total federal spending, while the bar graph would be better for directly comparing the amounts of money spent on these two programs.

In most cases, the work of interpreting information presented in graphs, tables, charts, and diagrams is done for the reader. The author will usually make explicit his or her reasons for presenting a certain set of data in such a way. However, an effective reader will avoid taking the author's claims for granted. Before considering the information presented in the graphic, the reader should consider whether the author has chosen the correct format for presentation, or whether the author has omitted variables or other information that might undermine his case. Interpreting the graphic itself is essentially an exercise in spotting trends. On a graph, for instance, the reader should be alert for how one variable responds to a change in the other. If education level increases, for example, does income increase as well? The same can be done for a table. Readers should be alert for values that break or exaggerate a trend; these may be meaningless outliers or indicators of a change in conditions.

When a reader is required to draw conclusions from the information presented in graphs, tables, charts, or diagrams, it is important to limit these conclusions to the terms of the graphic itself. In other words, the reader should avoid extrapolating from the data to make claims that are not supportable. As an example, consider a graph that compares the price of eggs to the demand. If the price and demand rise and fall together, a reader would be justified in saying that the demand for eggs and the price are tied together. However, this simple graph does not indicate which of these variables causes the other, so the reader would not be justified in concluding that the price of eggs raises or lowers the demand. In fact, demand could be tied to all sorts of other factors not included in this chart.

> **Review Video: Graphic Organizers**
> Visit mometrix.com/academy and enter code: 665513

Types of Tables and Charts

Tables are presented in a standard format so that they will be easy to read and understand. At the top of the table, there will be a title. This will be a short phrase indicating the information the table or graph intends to convey. The title of a table could be something like "Average Income for Various Education Levels" or "Price of Milk Compared to Demand." A table is composed of information laid out in vertical columns and horizontal rows. Typically, each column will have a label. If "Average Income for Various Education Levels" was placed in a table format, the two columns could be labeled "Education Level" and "Average Income." Each location on the table is called a cell. Cells are defined by their column and row (e.g., second column, fifth row). The table's information is placed in these cells.

Like a table, a **graph** will typically have a title on top. This title may simply state the identities of the two axes: e.g., "Income vs. Education." However, the title may also be something more descriptive, like "A comparison of average income with level of education." In any case, bar and line graphs are laid out along two perpendicular lines, or axes. The vertical axis is called the y-axis, and the horizontal axis is called the x-axis. It is typical for the x-axis to be the independent variable and the y-axis to be the dependent variable. The independent variable is the one manipulated by the researcher or whoever put together the graph. In the above example, the independent variable would be "level of education," since the maker of the graph will define these values (high school, college, master's degree, etc.). The dependent value is not controlled by the researcher.

When selecting a graph format, it is important to consider the intention and the structure of the presentation. A bar graph, for instance, is appropriate for displaying the relations between a series of distinct quantities that are on the same scale. For instance, if one wanted to display the amount of money spent on groceries during the months of a year, a bar graph would be appropriate. The vertical axis would represent values of money, and the horizontal axis would identify the bar representing each month. A line graph also requires data expressed in common units, but it is better for demonstrating the general trend in that data. If the grocery expenses were plotted on a line graph instead of a bar graph, there would be more emphasis on whether the amount of money spent rose or fell over the course of the year. Whereas a bar graph is good for showing the relationships between the different values plotted, the line graph is good for showing whether the values tended to increase, decrease, or remain stable.

A **line graph** is a type of graph that is typically used for measuring trends over time. It is set up along a vertical and a horizontal axis. The variables being measured are listed along the left side and the bottom side of the axes. Points are then plotted along the graph, such that they correspond with their values for each variable. For instance, imagine a line graph measuring a person's income for each month of the year. If the person earned $1500 in January, there would be a point directly above January, perpendicular to the horizontal axis, and directly to the right of $1500, perpendicular to the vertical axis. Once all of the lines are plotted, they are connected with a line from left to right. This line provides a nice visual illustration of the general trends. For instance, using the earlier example, if the line sloped up, it would be clear that the person's income had increased over the course of the year.

The **bar graph** is one of the most common visual representations of information. Bar graphs are used to illustrate sets of numerical data. The graph has a vertical axis, along which numbers are listed, and a horizontal axis, along which categories, words, or some other indicators are placed. One example of a bar graph is a depiction of the respective heights of famous basketball players: the vertical axis would contain numbers ranging from five to eight feet, and the horizontal axis would contain the names of the players. The length of the bar above the player's name would illustrate his height, as the top of the bar would stop perpendicular to the height listed along the left side. In this representation, then, it would be easy to see that Yao Ming is taller than Michael Jordan, because Yao's bar would be higher.

A **pie chart**, also known as a circle graph, is useful for depicting how a single unit or category is divided. The standard pie chart is a circle within which wedges have been cut and labeled. Each of these wedges is proportional in size to its part of the whole. For instance, consider a pie chart representing a student's budget. If the student spends half her money on rent, then the pie chart will represent that amount with a line through the center of the pie. If she spends a quarter of her money on food, there will be a line extending from the edge of the circle to the center at a right angle to the line depicting rent. This illustration would make it clear that the student spends twice as much money on rent as she does on food. The pie chart is only appropriate for showing how a whole is divided.

A pie chart is effective at showing how a single entity is divided into parts. They are not effective at demonstrating the relationships between parts of different wholes. For example, it would not be as helpful to use a pie chart to compare the respective amounts of state and federal spending devoted to infrastructure, since these values are only meaningful in the context of the entire budget.

Plot lines are another way to visual represent information. Every plot line follows the same stages. One can identify each of these stages in every story they read. These stages are: the introduction, rising action, conflict, climax, falling action, and resolution. The introduction tells the reader what the story will be about and sets up the plot. The rising action is what happens that leads up to the conflict, which is some sort of problem that arises, with the climax at its peak. The falling action is what happens after the climax of the conflict. The resolution is the conclusion and often has the final solution to the problem in the conflict. A plot line looks like this:

Review Video: Plot Line
Visit mometrix.com/academy and enter code: 944011

Determining Word Meaning

An understanding of the basics of language is helpful, and often vital, to understanding what you read. The term *structural analysis* refers to looking at the parts of a word and breaking it down into its different components to determine the word's meaning. Parts of a word include prefixes, suffixes, and the root word. By learning the meanings of prefixes, suffixes, and other word fundamentals, you can decipher the meaning of words which may not yet be in your vocabulary. Prefixes are common letter combinations at the beginning of words, while suffixes are common letter combinations at the end. The main part of the word is known as the root. Visually, it would look like this: prefix + root word + suffix. Look first at the individual meanings of the root word, prefix and/or suffix. Using knowledge of the meaning(s) of the prefix and/or suffix to see what information it adds to the root. Even if the meaning of the root is unknown, one can use knowledge of the prefix's and/or suffix's meaning(s) to determine an approximate meaning of the word. For example, if one sees the word *uninspired* and does not know what it means, they can use the knowledge that *un-* means 'not' to know that the full word means "not inspired." Understanding the common prefixes and suffixes can illuminate at least part of the meaning of an unfamiliar word.

Review Video: Determining Word Meanings
Visit mometrix.com/academy and enter code: 894894

Below is a list of common prefixes and their meanings:

Prefix	Definition	Examples
a	in, on, of, up, to	abed, afoot
a-	without, lacking	atheist, agnostic
ab-	from, away, off	abdicate, abjure
ad-	to, toward	advance
am-	friend, love	amicable, amatory
ante-	before, previous	antecedent, antedate
anti-	against, opposing	antipathy, antidote
auto-	self	autonomy, autobiography
belli-	war, warlike	bellicose

- 38 -

Prefix	Definition	Examples
bene-	well, good	benefit, benefactor
bi-	two	bisect, biennial
bio-	life	biology, biosphere
cata-	down, away, thoroughly	catastrophe, cataclysm
chron-	time	chronometer, synchronize
circum-	around	circumspect, circumference
com-	with, together, very	commotion, complicate
contra-	against, opposing	contradict, contravene
cred-	belief, trust	credible, credit
de-	from	depart
dem-	people	demographics, democracy
dia-	through, across, apart	diameter, diagnose
dis-	away, off, down, not	dissent, disappear
epi-	upon	epilogue
equi-	equal, equally	equivalent
ex-	out	extract
for-	away, off, from	forget, forswear
fore-	before, previous	foretell, forefathers
homo-	same, equal	homogenized
hyper-	excessive, over	hypercritical, hypertension
hypo-	under, beneath	hypodermic, hypothesis
in-	in, into	intrude, invade
in-	not, opposing	incapable, ineligible
inter-	among, between	intercede, interrupt
intra-	within	intramural, intrastate
magn-	large	magnitude, magnify
mal-	bad, poorly, not	malfunction
micr-	small	microbe, microscope
mis-	bad, poorly, not	misspell, misfire
mono-	one, single	monogamy, monologue
mor-	die, death	mortality, mortuary
neo-	new	neolithic, neoconservative
non-	not	nonentity, nonsense
ob-	against, opposing	objection
omni-	all, everywhere	omniscient
ortho-	right, straight	orthogonal, orthodox
over-	above	overbearing
pan-	all, entire	panorama, pandemonium
para-	beside, beyond	parallel, paradox
per-	through	perceive, permit
peri-	around	periscope, perimeter
phil-	love, like	philosophy, philanthropic
poly-	many	polymorphous, polygamous

Prefix	Definition	Examples
post-	after, following	postpone, postscript
pre-	before, previous	prevent, preclude
prim-	first, early	primitive, primary
pro-	forward, in place of	propel, pronoun
re-	back, backward, again	revoke, recur
retro-	back, backward	retrospect, retrograde
semi-	half, partly	semicircle, semicolon
sub-	under, beneath	subjugate, substitute
super-	above, extra	supersede, supernumerary
sym-	with, together	sympathy, symphony
trans-	across, beyond, over	transact, transport
ultra-	beyond, excessively	ultramodern, ultrasonic, ultraviolet
un-	not, reverse of	unhappy, unlock
uni-	one	uniform, unity
vis-	to see	visage, visible

Below is a list of common suffixes and their meanings:

Suffix	Definition	Examples
-able	able to, likely	capable, tolerable
-age	process, state, rank	passage, bondage
-ance	act, condition, fact	acceptance, vigilance
-arch	to rule	monarch
-ard	one that does excessively	drunkard, wizard
-ate	having, showing	separate, desolate
-ation	action, state, result	occupation, starvation
-cy	state, condition	accuracy, captaincy
-dom	state, rank, condition	serfdom, wisdom
-en	cause to be, become	deepen, strengthen
-er	one who does	teacher
-esce	become, grow, continue	convalesce, acquiesce
-esque	in the style of, like	picturesque, grotesque
-ess	feminine	waitress, lioness
-fic	making, causing	terrific, beatific
-ful	full of, marked by	thankful, zestful
-fy	make, cause, cause to have	glorify, fortify
-hood	state, condition	manhood, statehood
-ible	able, likely, fit	edible, possible, divisible
-ion	action, result, state	union, fusion
-ish	suggesting, like	churlish, childish
-ism	act, manner, doctrine	barbarism, socialism
-ist	doer, believer	monopolist, socialist
-ition	action, state, result	sedition, expedition
-ity	state, quality, condition	acidity, civility

Suffix	Definition	Examples
-ize	make, cause to be, treat with	sterilize, mechanize, criticize
-less	lacking, without	hopeless, countless
-like	like, similar	childlike, dreamlike
-logue	type of written/spoken language	prologue
-ly	like, of the nature of	friendly, positively
-ment	means, result, action	refreshment, disappointment
-ness	quality, state	greatness, tallness
-or	doer, office, action	juror, elevator, honor
-ous	marked by, given to	religious, riotous
-ship	the art or skill of	statesmanship
-some	apt to, showing	tiresome, lonesome
-th	act, state, quality	warmth, width
-tude	quality, state, result	magnitude, fortitude
-ty	quality, state	enmity, activity
-ward	in the direction of	backward, homeward

Review Video: English Root Words
Visit mometrix.com/academy and enter code: 896380

When defining words in a text, words often have a meaning that is more than the dictionary definition. The **denotative** meaning of a word is the literal meaning. The **connotative** meaning goes beyond the denotative meaning to include the emotional reaction a word may invoke. The connotative meaning often takes the denotative meaning a step further due to associations which the reader makes with the denotative meaning. The reader can differentiate between the denotative and connotative meanings by first recognizing when authors use each meaning. Most non-fiction, for example, is fact-based, the authors not using flowery, figurative language. The reader can assume that the writer is using the denotative, or literal, meaning of words. In fiction, on the other hand, the author may be using the connotative meaning. Connotation is one form of figurative language. The reader should use context clues to determine if the author is using the denotative or connotative meaning of a word.

Review Video: Denotation and Connotation
Visit mometrix.com/academy and enter code: 310092

Readers of all levels will encounter words with which they are somewhat unfamiliar. The best way to define a word in **context** is to look for nearby words that can help. For instance, unfamiliar nouns are often accompanied by examples that furnish a definition. Consider the following sentence: "Dave arrived at the party in hilarious garb: a leopard-print shirt, buckskin trousers, and high heels." If a reader was unfamiliar with the meaning of garb, he could read the examples and quickly determine that the word means "clothing." Examples will not always be this obvious. For instance, consider this sentence: "Parsley, lemon, and flowers were just a few of items he used as garnishes." Here, the possibly unfamiliar word *garnishes* is exemplified by parsley, lemon, and flowers. Readers who have eaten in a few restaurants will probably be able to identify a garnish as something used to decorate a plate.

Review Video: Context
Visit mometrix.com/academy and enter code: 613660

In addition to looking at the context of a passage, readers can often use contrasts to define an unfamiliar word in context. In many sentences, the author will not describe the unfamiliar word directly, but will instead describe the opposite of the unfamiliar word. Of course, this provides information about the word the reader needs to define. Consider the following example: "Despite his intelligence, Hector's low brow and bad posture made him look obtuse." The author suggests that Hector's appearance was opposite to his actual intelligence. Therefore, *obtuse* must mean unintelligent or stupid. Here is another example: "Despite the horrible weather, we were beatific about our trip to Alaska." The word *despite* indicates that the speaker's feelings were at odds with the weather. Since the weather is described as "horrible," *beatific* must mean something good.

In some cases, there will be very few contextual clues to help a reader define the meaning of an unfamiliar word. When this happens, one strategy the reader may employ is substitution. A good reader will brainstorm some possible synonyms for the given word, and then substitute these words into the sentence. If the sentence and the surrounding passage continue to make sense, the substitution has revealed at least some information about the unfamiliar word. Consider the sentence, "Frank's admonition rang in her ears as she climbed the mountain." A reader unfamiliar with *admonition* might come up with some substitutions like "vow," "promise," "advice," "complaint," or "compliment." All of these words make general sense of the sentence, though their meanings are diverse. The process has suggested, however, that an admonition is some sort of message. The substitution strategy is rarely able to pinpoint a precise definition, but can be effective as a last resort.

It is sometimes possible to define an unfamiliar word by looking at the descriptive words in the context. Consider the following sentence: "Fred dragged the recalcitrant boy kicking and screaming up the stairs." *Dragged*, *kicking*, and *screaming* all suggest that the boy does not want to go up the stairs. The reader may assume that *recalcitrant* means something like unwilling or protesting. In that example, an unfamiliar adjective was identified. It is perhaps more typical to use description to define an unfamiliar noun, as in this sentence: "Don's wrinkled frown and constantly shaking fist identified him as a curmudgeon of the first order." Don is described as having a "wrinkled frown and constantly shaking fist," suggesting that a *curmudgeon* must be a grumpy old man. Contrasts do not always provide detailed information about the unfamiliar word, but they at least give the reader some clues.

When a word has more than one meaning, it can be tricky to determine how it is being used in a given sentence. Consider the verb *cleave*, which bizarrely can mean either "join" or "separate." When a reader comes upon this word, she will have to select the definition that makes the most sense. So, take as an example the following sentence: "The birds cleaved together as they flew from the oak tree." Immediately, the presence of the word *together* should suggest that in this sentence *cleave* is being used to mean "*join*." A slightly more difficult example would be the sentence, "Hermione's knife cleaved the bread cleanly." It doesn't make sense for a knife to join bread together, so the word must be meant to indicate separation. Discovering the meaning of a word with multiple meanings requires the same tricks as defining an unknown word: looking for contextual clues and evaluating substituted words.

Literary Devices

Understanding how words relate to each other can often add meaning to a passage. This is explained by understanding **synonyms** (words that mean the same thing) and **antonyms** (words that mean the opposite of one another). As an example, *dry* and *arid* are synonyms, and *dry* and *wet* are antonyms. There are many pairs of words in English that can be considered synonyms, despite having slightly different definitions. For instance, the words *friendly* and *collegial* can both be used to describe a warm interpersonal relationship, so it would be correct to call them synonyms. However, *collegial* (kin to *colleague*) is more often used in reference to professional or academic relationships, while *friendly* has no such connotation. Nevertheless, it would be appropriate to call these words synonyms. If the difference between the two words is too great, however, they may not be called synonyms. *Hot* and *warm* are not synonyms, for instance, because their meanings are too distinct. A good way to determine whether two words are synonyms is to substitute one for the other and see if the sentence means the same thing. Substituting *warm* for *hot* in a sentence would convey a different meaning.

Antonyms are opposites. *Light* and *dark*, *up* and *down*, *right* and *left*, *good* and *bad*: these are all sets of antonyms. It is important to distinguish between antonyms and pairs of words that are simply different. *Black* and *gray*, for instance, are not antonyms because gray is not the opposite of black. *Black* and *white*, on the other hand, are antonyms. Not every word has an antonym. For instance, many nouns do not. What would be the antonym of *chair*, after all? On a standardized test, the questions related to antonyms are more likely to concern adjectives. Remember that adjectives are words that describe a noun. Some common adjectives include *red*, *fast*, *skinny*, and *sweet*. Of these four examples, only *red* lacks a group of obvious antonyms.

> **Review Video:** <u>Synonyms and Antonyms</u>
> Visit mometrix.com/academy and enter code: 105612

There are many types of language devices that authors use to convey their meaning in a more descriptive or interesting way. Understanding these concepts will help you understand what you read. These types of devices are called *figurative language* – language that goes beyond the literal meaning of the words. **Descriptive language** that evokes imagery in the reader's mind is one type of figurative language. **Exaggeration** is also one type of figurative language. Also, when you compare two things, you are using figurative language. **Similes** and **metaphors** are ways of comparing things, and both are types of figurative language commonly found in poetry. An example of figurative language (a simile in this case) is: "The child howled like a coyote when her mother told her to pick up the toys." In this example, the child's howling is compared to that of a coyote. Figurative language is descriptive in nature and helps the reader understand the sound being made in this sentence.

Alliteration is a stylistic device, or literary technique, in which successive words (more strictly, stressed syllables) begin with the same sound or letter. Alliteration is a frequent tool in poetry but it is also common in prose, particularly to highlight short phrases. An example of alliteration could be "thundering through the thickets," in which the initial th sound is used in four consecutive words. Especially in poetry, it contributes to euphony of the passage, lending it a musical air. It may act to humorous effect. Alliteration draws attention to itself, which may be a good or a bad thing. Authors should be conscious of the character of the sound to be repeated. In the above example, a *th* sound is somewhat difficult to make quickly in four consecutive words, so the phrase conveys a little of the difficulty of moving through tall grass. If the author is indeed trying to suggest this difficulty, then the alliteration is a success. Consider, however, the description of eyes as "glassy

- 43 -

globes of glitter." This is definitely alliteration, since the initial *gl* sound is used three times. However, one might question whether this awkward sound is appropriate for a description of pretty eyes. The phrase is not especially pleasant to the ear, and therefore is probably not effective as alliteration. Related to alliteration are *assonance*, the repetition of vowel sounds, and *consonance*, the repetition of consonant sounds.

> **Review Video: Alliteration**
> Visit mometrix.com/academy and enter code: 462837

A **figure of speech**, sometimes termed a rhetorical figure or device, or elocution, is a word or phrase that departs from straightforward, literal language. Figures of speech are often used and crafted for emphasis, freshness of expression, or clarity. However, clarity may also suffer from their use.

Note that not all theories of meaning necessarily have a concept of "literal language" (see literal and figurative language). Under theories that do not, figure of speech is not an entirely coherent concept.

As an example of the figurative use of a word, consider the sentence, "I am going to crown you." It may mean:

- I am going to place a literal crown on your head.
- I am going to symbolically exalt you to the place of kingship.
- I am going to punch you in the head with my clenched fist.
- I am going to put a second checker on top of your checker to signify that it has become a king.

> **Review Video: Figure of Speech**
> Visit mometrix.com/academy and enter code: 111295

A **metaphor** is a type of figurative language in which the writer equates one thing with a different thing. For instance, in the sentence "The bird was an arrow arcing through the sky," the arrow is serving as a metaphor for the bird. The point of a metaphor is to encourage the reader to think about the thing being described in a different way. Using this example, we are being asked to envision the bird's flight as being similar to the arc of an arrow, so we will imagine it to be swift, bending, etc. Metaphors are a way for the author to describe without being direct and obvious. Metaphors are a more lyrical and suggestive way of providing information. Note that the thing to which a metaphor refers will not always be mentioned explicitly by the author. For instance, consider the following description of a forest in winter: "Swaying skeletons reached for the sky and groaned as the wind blew through them." The author is clearly using *skeletons* as a metaphor for leafless trees. This metaphor creates a spooky tone while inspiring the reader's imagination.

> **Review Video: Metaphor**
> Visit mometrix.com/academy and enter code: 133295

Metonymy is referring to one thing in terms of another, closely related thing. This is similar to metaphor, but there is less distance between the description and the thing being described. An example of metonymy is referring to the news media as the "press," when of course the press is only the device by which newspapers are printed. Metonymy is a way of referring to something without having to repeat its name constantly. **Synecdoche**, on the other hand, is referring to a whole by one of its parts. An example of synecdoche would be calling a police officer a "badge." Synecdoche, like metonymy, is a handy way of referring without having to overuse certain words. It also allows the writer to emphasize aspects of the thing being described. For instance, referring to businessmen as "suits" suggests professionalism, conformity, and drabness.

Hyperbole is overstatement for effect. The following sentence is an example of hyperbole: *He jumped ten feet in the air when he heard the good news*. Obviously, no person has the ability to jump ten feet in the air. The author hyperbolizes not because he believes the statement will be taken literally, but because the exaggeration conveys the extremity of emotion. Consider how much less colorful the sentence would be if the author simply said, "He jumped when he heard the good news." Hyperbole can be dangerous if the author does not exaggerate enough. For instance, if the author wrote, "He jumped two feet in the air when he heard the good news," the reader might not be sure whether this is actually true or just hyperbole. Of course, in many situations this distinction will not really matter. However, an author should avoid confusing or vague hyperbole when he needs to maintain credibility or authority with readers.

Understatement is the opposite of hyperbole: that is, it is describing something as less than it is, for effect. As an example, consider a person who climbs Mount Everest and then describes the journey as "a little stroll." This is an almost extreme example of understatement. Like other types of figurative language, understatement has a range of uses. It may convey self-deprecation or modesty, as in the above example. Of course, some people might interpret understatement as false modesty, a deliberate attempt to call attention to the magnitude of what is being discussed. For example, a woman is complimented on her enormous diamond engagement ring and says, "Oh, this little thing?" Her understatement might be viewed as snobby or insensitive. Understatement can have various effects, but it always calls attention to itself.

> **Review Video: Hyperbole and Understatement**
> Visit mometrix.com/academy and enter code: 308470

A **simile** is a figurative expression similar to a metaphor, though it requires the use of a distancing word like *like* or *as*. Some examples are "The sun was like an orange," "eager as a beaver," and "nimble as a mountain goat." Because a simile includes *like* or a*s*, it creates a little space between the description and the thing being described. If an author says that a house was "like a shoebox," the tone is slightly different than if the author said that the house *was* a shoebox. In a simile, the author indicates an awareness that the description is not the same thing as the thing being described. In a metaphor, there is no such distinction, even though one may safely assume that the author is aware of it. This is a subtle difference, but authors will alternately use metaphors and similes depending on their intended tone.

> **Review Video: Simile**
> Visit mometrix.com/academy and enter code: 642949

Another type of figurative language is **personification.** This is the description of the nonhuman as if it were human. Literally, the word means the process of making something into a person. There is a wide range of approaches to personification, from common expressions like "whispering wind" to full novels like *Animal Farm*, by George Orwell, in which the Bolshevik Revolution is reenacted by farmyard animals. The general intent of personification is to describe things in a manner that will be comprehensible to readers. When an author states that a tree "groans" in the wind, she of course does not mean that the tree is emitting a low, pained sound from its mouth. Instead, she means that the tree is making a noise similar to a human groan. Of course, this personification establishes a tone of sadness or suffering. A different tone would be established if the author said the tree was "swaying" or "dancing."

Irony is a statement that suggests its opposite. In other words, it is when an author or character says one thing but means another. For example, imagine a man walks in his front door, covered in mud and in tattered clothes. His wife asks him, "How was your day?" and he says "Great!" The man's comment is an example of irony. As in this example, irony often depends on information the reader obtains elsewhere. There is a fine distinction between irony and sarcasm. Irony is any statement in which the literal meaning is opposite from the intended meaning, while sarcasm is a statement of this type that is also insulting to the person at whom it is directed. A sarcastic statement suggests that the other person is stupid enough to believe an obviously false statement is true. Irony is a bit more subtle than sarcasm.

The more words a person is exposed to, the greater their vocabulary will become. By reading on a regular basis, a person can increase the number of ways they have seen a word in context. Based on experience, a person can recall how a word was used in the past and apply that knowledge to a new context. For example, a person may have seen the word *gull* used to mean a bird that is found near the seashore. However, a *gull* can also be a person who is easily tricked. If the word is used in context in reference to a character, the reader can recognize that the character is being called a bird that is not seen as extremely intelligent. Using what the reader knows about a word can be useful when making comparisons or figuring out the meaning of a new use of a word, as in figurative language, idioms, analogies, and multiple-meaning words.

Writing

Choosing Topics

Very often the choice of a subject may be assigned or determined by someone besides the writer. When the choice is left to the writer, it is sometimes wise to allow the topic itself to "select" the writer. That is to say those topics that interest, engage, puzzle, or stimulate someone may be good choices. Engaging the writer is the most important factor in choosing a topic. Engagement notes a strong interest and spirit of inquiry about the subject. It is a signal that the subject and author are interacting in some creative sense, which usually encourages good writing. Even with an assigned topic, a particular aspect of the subject may interest the writer more than others. The key to any writer's choice of topic is the ability of a subject to inspire the author to question, speculate, inquire and interact. From this natural interest and attraction, some of the most creative writing develops.

A common problem is limiting the scope of a writing assignment. Narrowing the scope is not always enough, because the new subject may itself be too broad. Focusing on an aspect of a topic often effectively results in a topic both interesting and manageable. For example narrowing a topic like the "Civil War" to the "Battle of Antietam" may still leave an unwieldy topic. To sharpen the focus, an aspect such as "The use of artillery by Confederates at the battle of Antietam" could be selected.

Understanding Assignments

Many writing assignments address specific audiences (physicians, attorneys, and teachers) and have specific goals. These writers know for whom and why they are writing. This can clarify the writing significantly. Other assignments, particularly in academic settings, may appear with no specific subject, audience, or apparent purpose. Assignments may come with some variables; a specified audience, subject, or approach and leave the rest up to the writer. Because of these variables, it is useful to consider the following questions:

- What specifically is the assignment asking the writer to do?
- What information or knowledge is necessary to fulfill the assignment?
- Can the topic be broadened or limited to more effectively complete the project?
- Are there specific parameters or other requirements for the project?
- What is the purpose of the assignment?
- Who is the intended audience for the work?
- What is the length of the assignment? Does it limit or require a certain number of pages? If so, what are the parameters?
- What is the deadline for the assignment?   Sometimes preliminary materials are to be submitted before the main assignment. Considering these factors will give a writer information needed to set a schedule for the project.

Length and Document Design

Writers seldom have control over length and document design. Usually an academic assignment has a specified length, while journalists work within tight word count parameters. Document design often follows the purpose of a writing project. Specific formats are required for lab reports, research papers, and abstracts. The business world operates within fairly narrow format styles, the business letter, memo, and report allowing only a small departure from the standard format.

There are some assignments that allow the writer to choose the specific format for the work. The increased flourishes provided by computers allow a great deal of creativity in designing a visually stimulating and functional document. Improving readability is always a worthwhile goal for any project, and this is becoming much easier with available software.

Deadlines

Deadlines are a critical element in any writing assignment. They help a writer budget their time to complete the assignment on schedule. For elaborate or complex writing projects, it is useful to create a working schedule that includes time for research, writing, revising, and editing. Breaking the process down into more workable parts with their own deadlines, helps keep a writer aware of the progress being made.

Purposes of Writing

What is the main purpose of the proposed piece? This may be very clear and focused, or ambiguous. A writer should be clear about the purpose of his writing, as this will determine the direction and elements of the work. Generally purposes may be divided into three groups:

- To entertain.
- To persuade or convince.
- To educate or inform.

Some or all of these purposes may be the goal in a given writing assignment. It is helpful to try and identify the major purpose of a writing piece, as well as any secondary purposes involved. Purpose in writing must be linked closely to the writer's goals in undertaking the assignment. In academic settings, it is usually more accurate to think in terms of several goals. A student may wish to convince the audience in an entertaining and informative fashion. However one goal should be paramount. Expectations of the instructor play an important role in an academic assignment.

> **Review Video: Purpose**
> Visit mometrix.com/academy and enter code: 511819

Recursive Nature

The process of writing is described as recursive; This means that the goals and parts of the writing process are often a seamless flow, constantly influencing each other without clear boundaries. The "steps' in the writing process occur organically, with planning, drafting and revising all taking place simultaneously, in no necessary or orderly fashion. The writer rarely pays attention to the recursive patterns. The process unfolds naturally, without attention or dependence on a predetermined sequence. The writing process is a series of recursive activities, which rarely occur in a linear fashion, rather moving back and forth between planning, drafting, revising, more planning, more drafting, polishing until the writing is complete. Forthcoming topics will cover many parts of the process individually, but they go on together as a seamless flow.

> **Review Video: Recursive Writing Process**
> Visit mometrix.com/academy and enter code: 951611

Considering an Audience

The careful consideration of the anticipated audience is a requisite for any project. Although much of this work is intuitive, some guidelines are helpful in the analysis of an audience:

- Specifically identify your audience. Are they eclectic or share common characteristics?
- Determine qualities of the audience such as age, education, sex, culture, and special interests.
- Understand what the audience values; brevity, humor, originality, honesty are examples.
- What is the audience's attitude toward the topic; skeptical, knowledgeable, pro or con?
- Understand the writer's relationship to the audience; peer, authority, advocate, or antagonist?

Understanding the qualities of an audience allows the writer to form an organizational plan tailored to achieve the objectives of the writing with the audience in mind. It is essential to effective writing.

Level of Formality

In choosing a level of formality in writing, the subject and audience should be carefully considered. The subject may require a more dignified tone, or perhaps an informal style would be best. The relationship between writer and reader is important in choosing a level of formality. Is the audience one with which you can assume a close relationship, or should a more formal tone prevail?

Most student or business writing requires some degree of formality. Informal writing is appropriate for private letters, personal e-mails, and business correspondence between close associates. Vocabulary and language should be relatively simple.

It is important to be consistent in the level of formality in a piece of writing. Shifts in levels of formality can confuse readers and detract from the message of the writing.

Understanding the Topic

Easily overlooked is the basic question of ascertaining how knowledgeable the writer is about the subject. A careful evaluation should be made to determine what is known about the topic, and what information must be acquired to undertake the writing assignment. Most people have a good sense of how to go about researching a subject, using the obvious available resources: libraries, the internet, journals, research papers and other sources. There are however some specific strategies that can help a writer learn more about a subject, and just as importantly, what is not known and must be learned. These strategies or techniques not only are useful in researching a subject, they can also be used when problems come up during the actual writing phase of the assignment. These strategies include brainstorming, free writing, looping, and questioning.

Brainstorming

Brainstorming is a technique used frequently in business, industry, science, and engineering. It is accomplished by tossing out ideas, usually with several other people, in order to find a fresh approach or a creative way to approach a subject. This can be accomplished by an individual by simply free-associating about a topic. Sitting with paper and pen, every thought about the subject is written down in a word or phrase. This is done without analytical thinking, just recording what arises in the mind about the topic. The list is then read over carefully several times. The writer looks for patterns, repetitions, clusters of ideas, or a recurring theme. Although brainstorming can be done individually, it works best when several people are involved. Three to five people is ideal. This allows an exchange of ideas, points of view, and often results in fresh ideas or approaches.

Free Writing

Free writing is a form of brainstorming in a structured way. The method involves exploring a topic by writing about it for a certain period of time without stopping. A writer sets a time limit, and begins writing in complete sentences everything that comes to mind about the topic. Writing continues without interruption until the set period expires. When time expires, read carefully everything that has been written down. Much of it may make little or no sense, but insights and observations may emerge that the free writer did not know existed in his mind. Writing has a unique quality about it of jogging loose ideas, and seeing a word or idea appear may trigger others. Freewrtiting usually results in a fuller expression of ideas than brainstorming, because thoughts and associations are written in a more comprehensive manner. Both techniques can be used to complement one another and can yield much different results.

Looping

Looping is a variation of freewriting that focuses a topic in short five-minute stages, or loops. Looping is done as follows:

- With a subject in mind, spend five minutes freewriting without stopping. The results are the first loop.
- Evaluate what has been written in the first loop. Locate the strongest or most recurring thought which should be summarized in a single sentence. This is the "center of gravity", and is the starting point of the next loop.
- Using the summary sentence as a starting point, another five minute cycle of freewriting takes place. Evaluate the writing and locate the "center of gravity" for the second loop, and summarize it in a single sentence. This will be the start of the third loop.
- Continue this process until a clear new direction to the subject emerges. Usually this will yield a starting point for a whole new approach to a topic.

Looping can be very helpful when a writer is blocked or unable to generate new ideas on a subject.

Questioning

Asking and answering questions provides a more structured approach to investigating a subject. Several types of questions may be used to illuminate an issue.

- Questions to describe a topic. Questions such as "What is It?", "What caused it?", "What is it like or unlike?", "What is it a part of"? What do people say about it?" help explore a topic systematically.
- Questions to explain a topic. Examples include" Who, how, and what is it?", "Where does it end and begin?" What is at issue?", and "How is it done?"
- Questions to persuade include "What claims can be made about it?", "What evidence supports the claims?", "Can the claims be refuted?", and "What assumptions support the claims?"

Questioning can be a very effective device as it leads the writer through a process in a systematic manner in order to gain more information about a subject.

Thesis

A thesis states the main idea of the essay. A working or tentative thesis should be established early on in the writing process. This working thesis is subject to change and modification as writing progresses. It will serve to keep the writer focused as ideas develop.

The working thesis has two parts: a topic and a comment. The comment makes an important point about the topic. A working thesis should be interesting to an anticipated audience; it should be specific and limit the topic to a manageable scope. Theses three criteria are useful tools to measure the effectiveness of any working thesis. The writer applies these tools to ascertain:

- Is the topic of sufficient interest to hold an audience?
- Is the topic specific enough to generate interest?
- Is the topic manageable? Too broad? Too narrow? Can it be adequately researched?

Creating an effective thesis is an art. The thesis should be a generalization rather than a fact, and should be neither too broad or narrow in scope. A thesis prepares readers for facts and details, so it may not be a fact itself. It is a generalization that requires further proof or supporting points. Any thesis too broad may be an unwieldy topic and must be narrowed. The thesis should have a sharp focus, and avoid vague, ambivalent language. The process of bringing the thesis into sharp focus may help in outlining major sections of the work. This process is known as blueprinting, and helps the writer control the shape and sequence of the paper. Blueprinting outlines major points and supporting arguments that are used in elaborating on the thesis. A completed blueprint often leads to a development of an accurate first draft of a work. Once the thesis and opening are complete, it is time to address the body of the work.

> **Review Video: Thesis Statements**
>
> Visit mometrix.com/academy and enter code: 691033

Formal Outlines

A formal outline may be useful if the subject is complex, and includes many elements. here is a guide to preparing formal outlines:

- Always put the thesis at the top so it may be referred to as often as necessary during the outlining.
- Make subjects similar in generality as parallel as possible in the formal outline.
- Use complete sentences rather than phrases or sentence fragments in the outline.
- Use the conventional system of letters and numbers to designate levels of generality.
- There should be at least two subdivisions for each category in the formal outline.
- Limit the number of major sections in the outline. If there are too many major sections, combine some of them and supplement with additional sub-categories.
- Remember the formal outline is still subject to change; remain flexible throughout the process.

Research

Research is a means of critical inquiry, investigations based on sources of knowledge. Research is the basis of scientific knowledge, of inventions, scholarly inquiry, and many personal and general decisions. Much of work consists of research - finding something out and reporting on it. We can list five basic precepts about research:

- Everyone does research. To buy an car, go to a film, to investigate anything is research. We all have experience in doing research.
- Good research draws a person into a "conversation" about a topic. Results are more knowledge about a subject, understanding different sides to issues, and be able to discuss intelligently nuances of the topic.
- Research is always driven by a purpose. Reasons may vary from solving a problem to advocating a position, but research is almost always goal oriented.
- Research is shaped by purpose, and in turn the fruits of research refine the research further.
- Research is usually not a linear process; it is modified and changed by the results it yields.

Many writing assignments require research. Research is basically the process of gathering information for the writer's use. There are two broad categories of research:

1. Library research should be started after a research plan is outlined. Topics that require research should be listed, and catalogues, bibliographies, periodical indexes checked for references. Librarians are usually an excellent source of ideas and information on researching a topic.
2. Field research is based on observations, interviews, and questionnaires. This can be done by an individual or a team, depending on the scope of the field research.

The specific type and amount of research will vary widely with the topic and the writing assignment. A simple essay or story may require only a few hours of research, while a major project can consume weeks or months.

Research Material
- Primary sources are the raw material of research. This can include results of experiments, notes, and surveys or interviews done by the researcher. Other primary sources are books, letters, diaries, eyewitness accounts, and performances attended by the researcher.
- Secondary sources consist of oral and written accounts prepared by others. This includes reports, summaries, critical reviews, and other sources not developed by the researcher.

Most research writing uses both primary and secondary sources. Primary sources from first-hand accounts and secondary sources for background and supporting documentation. The research process calls for active reading and writing throughout. As research yields information, it often calls for more reading and research, and the cycle continues.

Organizing Information
Organizing information effectively is an important part of research. The data must be organized in a useful manner so that it can be effectively used. Three basic ways to organize information are:

1. Spatial organization - this is useful as it lets the user "see" the information, to fix it in space. This has benefits for those individuals who are visually adept at processing information.
2. Chronological organization is the most common presentation of information. This method places information in the sequence with which it occurs. Chronological organization is very useful in explaining a process that occurs in a step-by-step pattern.

3. Logical organization includes presenting material in a logical pattern that makes intuitive sense. Some patterns that are frequently used are illustrated, definition, compare/contrast, cause/effect, problem/solution, and division/classification. Each of these methods is discussed next.

Logical Organization

There are six major types of logical organization that are frequently used:

1. Illustrations may be used to support the thesis. Examples are the most common form of this organization.
2. Definitions say what something is or is not is another way of organization. What are the characteristics of the topic?
3. Dividing or classifying information into separate items according to their similarities is a common and effective organizing method.
4. Comparing, focusing on the similarities of things, and contrasting, highlighting the differences between things is an excellent tool to use with certain kinds of information.
5. Cause and effect is a simple tool to logically understand relationships between things. A phenomenon may be traced to its causes for organizing a subject logically.
6. Problem and solution is a simple and effective manner of logically organizing material. It is very commonly used and lucidly presents information.

Writing

An Initial Plan

After information gathering has been completed and the fruits of the research organized effectively, the writer now has a rough or initial plan for the work. A rough plan may be informal, consisting of a few elements such as "Introduction, Body, and Conclusions", or a more formal outline. The rough plan may include multiple organizational strategies within the over-all piece, or it may isolate one or two that can be used exclusively. At this stage the plan is just that, a rough plan subject to change as new ideas appear, and the organization takes a new approach. In these cases, the need for more research sometimes becomes apparent, or existing information should be considered in a new way. A more formal outline leads to an easier transition to a draft, but it can also limit the new possibilities that may arise as the plan unfolds. Until the outlines of the piece become clear, it is usually best to remain open to possible shifts in approaching the subject.

Supporting the Thesis

It is most important that the thesis of the paper be clearly expounded and adequately supported by additional points. The thesis sentence should contain a clear statement of the major theme and a comment about the thesis. The writer has an opportunity here to state what is significant or noteworthy of this particular treatment of the subject. Each sentence and paragraph in turn, should build on the thesis and support it.

Particular attention should be paid to insuring the organization properly uses the thesis and supporting points. It can be useful to outline the draft after writing, to insure that each paragraph leads smoothly to the next, and that the thesis is continually supported. The outline may highlight a weakness in flow or ideation that can be repaired. It will also spatially illustrate the flow of the argument, and provide a visual representation of the thesis and its supporting points. Often things become clearer when outlined than with a block of writing.

First Draft

Drafting is a mysterious art, and does not easily lend itself to rules. Generally, the more detailed the formal or informal outline, the easier is the transition to a first draft. The process of drafting is a learning one, and planning, organizing, and researching may be ongoing. Drafting is an evaluative process as well, and the whole project will be under scrutiny as the draft develops. The scope may be narrowed or widened, the approach may change, and different conclusions may emerge.

The process itself is shaped by the writer's preferences for atmosphere during the writing process. Time of day or night, physical location, ambient conditions, and any useful rituals can all play into the writer's comfort and productivity. The creation of an atmosphere conducive to the writer's best work is a subtle but important aspect of writing that is often overlooked. Although excellent writing has often been done in difficult situations, it is not the best prescription for success.

Evaluating the Draft

Once a draft is finished, an evaluation is in order. This can often mean reviewing the entire process with a critical eye. There is no formal checklist that insures a complete and effective evaluation, but there are some elements that can be considered:

- It should be determined whether sufficient research was done to properly develop the assignment. Are there areas that call for additional information? If so, what type?
- What are the major strengths of the draft? Are there any obvious weaknesses? How can these be fixed?
- Who is the audience for this work and how well does the material appeal to them?
- Does the material actually accomplish the goals of the assignment? If not, what needs to be done?

This is a stage for stepping back from the project and giving it an objective evaluation. Changes made now can improve the material significantly. Take time here to formulate a final approach to the subject.

Objective Criticism

Now is the time to obtain objective criticisms of the draft. It is helpful to provide readers with a list of questions to be answered about the draft. Some examples of effective questions are:

- Does the introduction catch the reader's attention? How can it be improved?
- Is the thesis clearly stated and supported by additional points?
- What type of organizational plan is used? Is it appropriate for the subject?
- Are paragraphs well developed and is there a smooth transition between them?
- Are the sentences well written and convey the appropriate meaning?
- Are words used effectively and colorfully in the text?
- What is the tone of the writing? Is it appropriate to the audience and subject?
- Is the conclusion satisfactory? Is there a sense of completion that the work is finished?
- What are main strengths and weaknesses of the writing? Are there specific suggestions for improvement?

Title, Introduction, and Conclusion

- A good title can identify the subject, describe it in a colorful manner, and give clues to the approach and sometimes conclusion of the writing. It usually defines the work in the mind of the reader.

- A strong introduction follows the lead of the title; it draws the readers into the work, and clearly states the topic with a clarifying comment. A common style is to state the topic, and then provide additional details, finally leading to a statement of the thesis at the end. An introduction can also begin with an arresting quote, question, or strong opinion, which grabs the reader's attention.
- A good conclusion should leave readers satisfied and provide a sense of closure. Many conclusions restate the thesis and formulate general statements that grow out of it. Writers often find ways to conclude in a dramatic fashion, through a vivid image, quotation, or a warning. This in an effort to give the ending the "punch" to tie up any existing points.

An introduction announces the main point of the work. It will usually be a paragraph of 50 to 150 words, opening with a few sentences to engage the reader, and conclude with the essay's main point. The sentence stating the main point is called the thesis. If possible, the sentences leading to the thesis should attract the reader's attention with a provocative question, vivid image, description, paradoxical statement, quotation, anecdote, or a question. The thesis could also appear at the beginning of the introduction. There are some types of writing that do not lend themselves to stating a thesis in one sentence. Personal narratives and some types of business writing may be better served by conveying an overriding purpose of the text, which may or may not be stated directly. The important point is to impress the audience with the rationale for the writing.

The body of the essay should fulfill the promise of the introduction and thesis. If an informal outline has not been done, now is the time for a more formal one. Constructing the formal outline will create a "skeleton" of the paper. Using this skeleton, it is much easier to fill out the body of an essay. It is useful to block out paragraphs based on the outline, to insure they contain all the supporting points, and are in the appropriate sequence.

The conclusion of the essay should remind readers of the main point, without belaboring it. It may be relatively short, as the body of the text has already "made the case" for the thesis. A conclusion can summarize the main points, and offer advice or ask a question. Never introduce new ideas in a conclusion. Avoid vague and desultory endings, instead closing with a crisp, often positive, note. A dramatic or rhetorical flourish can end a piece colorfully.

Examining Paragraphs

Paragraphs are a key structural unit of prose utilized to break up long stretches of words into more manageable subsets, and to indicate a shift in topics or focus. Each paragraph may be examined by identifying the main point of the section, and insuring that every sentence supports or relates to the main theme. Paragraphs may be checked to make sure the organization used in each is appropriate, and that the number of sentences are adequate to develop the topic.

Examining Sentences

Sentences are the building blocks of the written word, and they can be varied by paying attention to sentence length, sentence structure, and sentence openings. These elements should be varied so that writing does not seem boring, repetitive, or choppy. A careful analysis of a piece of writing will expose these stylistic problems, and they can be corrected before the final draft is written. Varying sentence structure and length can make writing more inviting and appealing to a reader.

Examining Words

A writer's choice of words is a signature of their style. A careful analysis of the use of words can improve a piece of writing. Attention to the use of specific nouns rather than general ones can enliven language. Verbs should be active whenever possible to keep the writing stronger and energetic, and there should be an appropriate balance between numbers of nouns and verbs. Too many nouns can result in heavy, boring sentences.

Examining Tone

Tone may be defined as the writer's attitude toward the topic, and to the audience. This attitude is reflected in the language used in the writing. If the language is ambiguous, tone becomes very difficult to ascertain. The tone of a work should be appropriate to the topic and to the intended audience. Some writing should avoid slang and jargon, while it may be fine in a different piece. Tone can range from humorous, to serious, and all levels in between. It may be more or less formal depending on the purpose of the writing, and its intended audience. All these nuances in tone can flavor the entire writing and should be kept in mind as the work evolves.

Tone is distinguished from mood, which is the feeling the writing evokes. Tone and mood may often be similar, but can also be significantly different. Mood often depends on the manner in which words and language are employed by the writer. In a sense tone and mood are two sides of a coin which color and language enliven the total approach of a writer to his subject. Mood and tone add richness and texture to words, bringing them alive in a deliberate strategy by the writer.

Examining Point-of-View

Point-of-view is the perspective from which writing occurs. There are several possibilities:

- First Person - Is written so that the "I" of the story is a participant or observer.
- Second Person - Is a device to draw the reader in more closely. It is really a variation or refinement of the first person narrative.
- Third Person - The most traditional form of third-person point-of-view is the "omniscient narrator", in which the narrative voice, (presumed to be the writer), is presumed to know everything about the characters, plot, and action. Most novels use this point-of-view.
- A Multiple Point-Of-View - The narration is delivered from the perspective of several characters.

In modern writing, the "stream-of consciousness" technique developed fully by James Joyce where the interior monologue provides the narration through the thoughts, impressions, and fantasies of the narrator.

Voice

Writers should find an appropriate voice that is appropriate for the subject, appeals to the intended audience, and conforms to the conventions of the genre in which the writing is done. If there is doubt about the conventions of the genre, lab reports, informal essays, research papers, business memos, and so on - a writer may examine models of these works written by experts in the field. These models can serve as examples for form and style for a particular type of writing.

Voice can also include the writer's attitude toward the subject and audience. Care should be taken that the language and tone of the writing is considered in terms of the purpose of the writing and it intended audience.

Gauging the appropriate voice for a piece is part art, and part science. It can be a crucial element in the ultimate effectiveness of the writing.

Writing Conventions

Conventions in writing are traditional assumptions or practices used by authors of all types of text. Some basic conventions have survived through the centuries - for example the assumption that a first person narrator in a work is telling the truth - others such as having characters in melodramas speak in asides to the audience have become outmoded. Conventions are particularly important in specialized types of writing which demand specific formats and styles. This is true of scientific and research papers, as well as much of academic and business writing. This formality has relaxed somewhat in several areas but still holds true for many fields of technical writing. Conventions are particularly useful for writers working in various types of nonfiction writing, where guidelines help the writer conform to the rules expected for that field. Conventions are part of the unspoken contract between writer and audience, and should be respected.

Writing Preparation

Effective writing requires preparation. The planning process includes everything done prior to drafting. Depending on the project, this could take a few minutes or several months. Elements in planning, and include considering the purpose of the writing, exploring a topic, developing a working thesis, gathering necessary materials, and developing a plan for organizing the writing. The organizational plan may vary in length and components, from a detailed outline or a stack of research cards. The organizational plan is a guide to help draft a writing project, and may change as writing progresses, but having a guide to refer to can keep a project on track. Planning is usually an ongoing process throughout the writing, but it is essential to begin with a structure.

Editing

Time must always be allowed for thorough and careful editing in order to insure clean and error-free work. It is helpful to create a checklist of editing to use as the manuscript is proofed. Patterns of editing problems often become apparent and understanding these patterns can eliminate them. Examples of patterns of errors include misuse of commas, difficulty in shifting tenses, and spelling problems. Once these patterns are seen, it is much easier to avoid them in the original writing. A checklist should be prepared based on every piece of writing, and should be cumulative. In this manner, progress may be checked regularly and the quantity and type of errors should be reduced over time. It is often helpful to have peer proof a manuscript, to get a fresh set of eyes on the material. Editing should be treated as an opportunity to polish and perfect a written work, rather than a chore that must be done. A good editor usually turns into a better writer over time.

Proofreading

As a proofreader, the goal is always to eliminate all errors. This includes typographical errors as well as any inconsistencies in spelling and punctuation. Begin by reading the prose aloud, calling out all punctuation marks and insuring that all sentences are complete and no words are left out. It is helpful to read the material again, backwards, so the focus is on each individual word, and the tendency to skip ahead is avoided.

A computer is a blessing to writers who have trouble proofreading their work. Spelling and grammar check programs may be utilized to reduce errors significantly. However it is still important for a writer to do the manual proofing necessary to insure errors of pattern are not repeated. Computers are a wonderful tool for writers but they must be employed by the writer, rather than as the writer. Skillful use of computers should result in a finely polished manuscript free of errors.

Review Video: General Revision and Proofreading
Visit mometrix.com/academy and enter code: 385882

Reviewers

Many professional and business writers work with editors who provide advice and support throughout the writing process. In academic situations, the use of reviewers is increasing, either by instructors or perhaps at an academic writing center. Peer review sessions are sometimes scheduled for class, and afford an opportunity to hear what other students feel about a piece of writing. This gives a writer a chance to serve as a reviewer.

Perspective

Textual Perspective

A textual knowledge of literature implies readers are taking a perspective or stance on the text. They are examining ways in which separate parts of the text relate to its overall form or structure. Textual perspectives must be used as a part of overall learning, not as an isolated feature. Textual perspective alone excludes both the author's life and the emotional experiences and attitudes of the reader. It fails to account for the readers' prior knowledge in their engagement with the work. A textual approach may include the ways in which the text shapes students' experience and emotional engagement. Based on previous reading, social acculturation, attitudes, and a host of other factors, students bring a wealth of information into any encounter with a text. Students may compare and contrast elements of their text with other works they have read or seen to form a more rounded engagement with a work.

Social Perspective

A rich resource for students' of literature is their own developing social knowledge. For adolescent students', social relationships are of primary importance. It is common for younger students' to impose their own social attitudes on a text, which is fertile ground for exploring how the understanding of texts is colored by social attitudes and experiences. Student's attitudes can help them reflect on the characters in a work, and can determine their relationship with the text itself.

Social perspectives can shed light on a number of important ways which can effect a reader's engagement with the text. A skillful teacher may probe these attitudes and experiences and make students' more aware of the impact of social attitudes to reading and studying a work of literature. This knowledge can become cumulative and promote more careful understanding of a literature over a period of time.

Cultural and Historical Context

The cultural knowledge and background of readers effects their response to texts. They can relate the works in a context of subcultures such as peer group, mass media, school, religion, and politics, social and historical communities. Engaging with the texts, readers can better understand how characters and authors are shaped by cultural influences. Cultural elements influence reader's reactions to events, including their responses to literature.

Cultural and historical context is important in understanding the roles of women and minorities in literature. Placing works of literature in their proper cultural setting can make a work more understandable and provoke reader interest in the milieu of the day. These factors can stimulate a reader's interest in how their own cultural background impacts the engagement with the text. Thus, the cultural aspects of literature become an opportunity for the reader to gain insight into their own attitudes.

Topical Perspective

In using a topical perspective, students apply their background in a variety of different fields, for instance sports, science, politics or cooking, to the literary work they are studying. Students may then engage the text in a holistic manner, bringing all their knowledge to bear on a work. It is useful to encourage students to determine how their own information pool relates to the work. There are an infinite number of fields or topics that relate to literature.

Students are most likely to integrate topics they are currently studying into their engagement with a text. These topics would include history, science, art, and music among others. Thinking about literature from these other topical point-of-view can help students ' understand that what they are learning in other courses enhances their experience of both literature and life.

Effects of Prior Knowledge

History

When students employ topical knowledge of history in their study of literature, they may do much more than remember date, events, and historical figures in relation to a text. They may well apply what they know about a historical period to better understand the attitudes and relationships in a work of literature. Students learn to think historically, considering different explanations for events, or cause and effect relationships in tracing a sequence of events. For example in reading Steinbeck's novels, students may draw on what they know about the historical period of the depression. Hemingway's "Farewell To Arms" may evoke a historical picture of Europe embroiled in World War I.

Literature offers an opportunity to apply historical knowledge in the context of a work. Students understand that both literary and historical accounts of an event or character may differ significantly, and that one may illuminate the other.

Scientific Knowledge

Students can apply their knowledge of science when reading literature. Their description of carefully observed phenomena can be used to describe a piece of writing. after reading essays by science writers, students' may be encouraged to transpose this knowledge into reading other texts. Understanding the scientific method gives readers' an opportunity to impose this process on events narrated in literature. The validity of events may be tested in the students' mind to assess the "reality" of the text.

There are many texts that take as their subject the role of the scientist in society. In reading "Frankenstein" or "Dr. Faustus", many issues can be raised about the responsibilities of scientists in conducting experiments.

The blending of science and literature is particularly compelling to some students' when they read science fiction or futuristic texts. An example would be "1984" which posits a authoritarian government controlling the lives of people.

Research Papers

<u>Hypothesis</u>

The result of a focusing process is a research question, a question or problem that can be solved by through research data. A hypothesis is a tentative answer to the research question that must be supported by the research. A research question must be manageable, specific, and interesting. Additionally, it must be argumentative, capable of being proved or disproved by research.

It is helpful to explore a topic with background reading and notes before formulating a research question and a hypothesis. Create a data base where all the knowledge of a topic is written down to be utilized in approaching the task of identifying the research question. This background work will allow a narrowing to a specific question, and formulate a tentative answer, the hypothesis. The process of exploring a topic can include brainstorming, freewriting, and scanning your memory and experience for information.

<u>Observing Data</u>

Collecting data in the field begins with direct observation, noting phenomena in a totally objective manner, and recording it. This requires a systematic approach to observation and recording information. Prior to beginning the observation process, certain steps must be accomplished:

- Determine the purpose of the observation and review the research question and hypothesis to see that they relate to each other
- Set a limited time period for the observations
- Develop a system for recording information in a useful manner
- Obtain proper materials for taking notes
- Consider the use of cameras, video recorders, or audio tape recorders
- Use the journalistic technique of asking "who, what, where, when, and why" to garner information

<u>Research Interviews</u>

After determining the exact purpose of the interview, check it against the research question and hypothesis. Set up the interview in advance, specifying the amount of time needed. Prepare a written list of questions for the interview, and try out questions on peers before the interview. Prepare a copy of your questions leaving room for notes. Insure that all the necessary equipment is on hand, and record the date, time, and subject of the interview.

The interview should be businesslike, and take only the allotted time. A flexible attitude will allow for questions or comments that have not been planned for, but may prove helpful to the process. Follow-up questions should be asked whenever appropriate. A follow-up thank you note is always appreciated and may pave the way for further interviews. Be mindful at all times of the research question and hypothesis under consideration.

<u>Surveys</u>

Surveys are usually in the form of questionnaires which have the advantage of speed and rapid compilation of data. Preparation of the questionnaire is of critical importance. Tie the questionnaire to the research question as closely as possible, and include questions which will bear on the hypothesis. Questions that can be answered "yes" or "no" can be easily tabulated. The following checklist may be helpful:

- Determine the audience for the questionnaire and how best to reach them
- Draft questions that will provide short, specific answers
- Test the questions on friends or peers
- Remember to include a deadline for return of the questionnaire
- Format the questionnaire so that it is clear and easily completed
- Carefully proofread the questionnaire and insure that it is neatly reproduced

Library Research

After reviewing personal resources for information, the library is the next stop. Use index cards or notepads for documentation. Create a system for reviewing data. It is helpful to create "key words" to trigger responses from sources. Some valuable guidelines for conducting library research include:

- Consult the reference librarian for sources and ideas.
- Select appropriate general and specific reference books for examination. Encyclopedias are a good place to start. There are numerous specialized encyclopedias to assist in research.
- Survey biographical dictionaries and indexes for information.
- Review almanacs, yearbooks, and statistical data.
- Scan periodical indexes for articles on the research topic.
- Determine if there are specialized indexes and abstracts that may be helpful.
- Review the computer or card catalog for relevant references.

Drafting the Research Essay

Before beginning the research essay, revisit the purpose, audience, and scope of the essay. An explicit thesis statement should summarize major arguments and approaches to the subject. After determining the special format of the essay, a survey of the literature on the subject is helpful. If original or first-hand research is involved, a summary of the methods and conclusions should be prepared.

A clustering strategy assembles all pertinent information on a topic in one physical place. The preparation of an outline may be based on the clusters, or a first draft may be developed without an outline. Formal outlines use a format of "Thesis statement", "Main topic", and "Supporting ideas" to shape the information. Drafting the essay can vary considerably among researchers, but it is useful to use an outline or information clusters to get started. Drafts are usually done on a point-to-point basis.

Introduction

The introduction to a research essay is particularly important as it sets the context for the essay. It needs to draw the reader into the subject, and also provide necessary background to understand the subject. It is sometimes helpful to open with the research question, and explain how the question will be answered. The major points of the essay may be forecast or previewed to prepare readers for the coming arguments.

In a research essay it is a good idea to establish the writer's credibility by reviewing credentials and experience with the subject. Another useful opening involves quoting several sources that support the points of the essay, again to establish credibility. The tone should be appropriate to the audience and subject, maintaining a sense of careful authority while building the arguments. Jargon should be kept to a minimum, and language carefully chosen to reflect the appropriate tone.

Conclusion

The conclusion to a research essay helps readers' summarize what they have learned. Conclusions are not meant to convince, as this has been done in the body of the essay. It can be useful to leave the reader with a memorable phrase or example that supports the argument. Conclusions should be both memorable but logical restatements of the arguments in the body of the essay.

A specific-to-general pattern can be helpful, opening with the thesis statement and expanding to more general observations. A good idea is to restate the main points in the body of the essay, leading to the conclusion. An ending that evokes a vivid image or asks a provocative question makes the essay memorable. The same effect can be achieved by a call for action, or a warning. Conclusions may be tailored to the audience's background, both in terms of language, tone, and style.

Reviewing the Draft

A quick checklist for reviewing a draft of a research essay includes:

- Introduction - Is the reader's attention gained and held by the introduction?
- Thesis - Does the essay fulfill the promise of the thesis? Is it strong enough?
- Main Points - List the main points and rank them in order of importance.
- Organization - What is the organizing principle of the essay? Does it work?
- Supporting Information - Is the thesis adequately supported? Is the thesis convincing?
- Source Material - Are there adequate sources and are they smoothly integrated into the essay?
- Conclusion - Does the conclusion have sufficient power? Does it summarize the essay well?
- Paragraphs, Sentences, and Words - Review all these for effectiveness in promoting the thesis.
- Overall Review - Evaluate the essay's strengths and weaknesses. What revisions are needed?

Modern Language Association Style

The Modern Language Association style is widely used in literature and languages as well as other fields. The MLA style calls for noting brief references to sources in parentheses in the text of an essay, and adding an alphabetical list of sources, called "Works Cited", at the end. Specific recommendations of the MLA include:

- Works Cited - Includes only works actually cited. List on a separate page with the author's name, title, and publication information, which must list the location of the publisher, the publishers' name, and the date of publication.
- Parenthetical Citations - MLA style uses parenthetical citations following each quotation, reference, paraphrase, or summary to a source. Each citation is made up of the author's last name and page reference, keyed to a reference in "Works Cited".
- Explanatory Notes - Explanatory notes are numbered consecutively, and identified by superscript numbers in the text. The full notes may appear as endnotes or as footnotes at the bottom of the page.

American Psychological Association Style

The American Psychological Association style is widely followed in the social sciences. The APA parenthetical citations within the text directs readers to a list of sources. In APA style this list is called "References". References are listed on a separate page, and each line includes the author's name, publication date, title, and publication information. Publication information includes the city where the publisher is located, and the publisher's name. Underline the titles of books and periodicals, but not articles.

APA parenthetical expressions citations include the author's last name, the date of publication, and the page number. APA style allows for content footnotes for information needed to be expanded or supplemented, marked in the text by superscript numbers in consecutive order. Footnotes are listed under a separate page, headed "Footnotes" after the last page of text. All entries should be double-spaced.

Revisions

Revising Sentences

Revising sentences is done to make writing more effective. Editing sentences is done to correct any errors. Revising sentences is usually best done on a computer, where it is possible to try several versions easily. Some writers prefer to print out a hard copy and work with this for revisions. Each works equally well and depends on the individual preference.

Spelling and grammar checks on software are a great aid to a writer but not a panacea. Many grammatical problems, such as faulty parallelism, mixed constructions, and misplaced modifiers can slip past the programs. Even if errors are caught, the writing still must be evaluated for effectiveness. A combination of software programs and writer awareness is necessary to insure an error free manuscript.

Global Revisions

Global revisions address the larger elements of writing. They usually affect paragraphs or sections, and may involve condensing or merging sections of text to improve meaning and flow. Sometimes material may be rearranged to better present the arguments of the essay. It is usually better for the writer to get some distance from the work before starting a global revision. Reviewers and editors can be usefully employed to make suggestions for revision. If reviewers are utilized, it is helpful to emphasize the focus on the larger themes of the work, rather than the finer points. When undertaking a global review, the writer might wish to position himself as the audience, rather than the writer. This provides some additional objectivity, and can result in a more honest appraisal of the writing and revisions that should be made. Global revisions are the last major changes a writer will make in the text. seal to persuade, inform, or entertain them. Answering these questions as objectively as possible will allow for a useful global revision.

- Purpose - Does the draft accomplish its purpose? Is the material and tone appropriate for the intended audience? Does it account for the audience's knowledge of the subject? Does it seek to persuade, inform, or entertain them?
- Focus - Does the introduction and the conclusion focus on the main point? Are all supporting arguments focused on the thesis?
- Organization and Paragraphing - Are there enough organizational cues to guide the reader? Are any paragraphs too long or too short?

- Content - Is the supporting material persuasive? Are all ideas adequately developed? Is there any material that could be deleted?
- Point -of-view - Is the draft free of distracting sifts in point-of-view? Is the point-of-view appropriate for the subject and intended audience?

Paragraphs

A paragraph should be unified around a main point. A good topic sentence summarizing the paragraphs main point. A topic sentence is more general than subsequent supporting sentences. Sometime the topic sentence will be used to close the paragraph if earlier sentences give a clear indication of the direction of the paragraph. Sticking to the main point means deleting or omitting unnecessary sentences that do not advance the main point.

The main point of a paragraph deserves adequate development, which usually means a substantial paragraph. A paragraph of two or three sentences often does not develop a point well enough, particularly if the point is a strong supporting argument of the thesis. An occasional short paragraph is fine, particularly it is used as a transitional device. A choppy appearance should be avoided.

Methods of development:

- **Examples** are a common method of development and may be effectively used when a reader may ask "For Example?" Examples are selected instances, not an inclusive catalog. They may be used to suggest the validity of topic sentences.
- **Illustrations** are extended examples, sometimes presented in story form for interest. They usually require several sentences each, so they are used sparingly. Well selected illustrations can be a colorful and vivid way of developing a point.
- **Stories** that command reader interest, developed in a story form, can be powerful methods of emphasizing key points in a essay. Stories and illustrations should be very specific and relate directly to a point or points being made in the text. They allow more colorful language and instill a sense of human interest in a subject. Used judiciously, illustrations and stories are an excellent device.
- **Analogies** draw comparisons between items that appear to have nothing in common. Analogies are employed by writers to attempt to provoke fresh thoughts and changed feelings about a subject. They may be used to make the unfamiliar more familiar, to clarify an abstract point, or to argue a point. Although analogies are effective literary devices, they should be used thoughtfully in arguments. Two things may be alike in some respects but completely different in others.
- **Cause and effect** is a excellent device and are best used when the cause and effect are generally accepted as true. As a matter of argument, cause and effect is usually too complex and subject to other interpretations to be used effectively. A valid way of using cause and effect is to state the effect in the topic sentence of a paragraph, and add the causes in the body of the paragraph. This adds logic and form to a paragraph, and usually makes it more effective.

Types of paragraphs:

- A paragraph of narration tells a story or part of a story. They are usually arranged in chronological order, but sometimes include flashbacks, taking the story back to an earlier time.

- A descriptive paragraph paints a verbal portrait of a person, place, or thing, using specific details that appeal to one or more of our senses - sight, sound, smell, taste, and touch. It conveys a real sense of being present and observing phenomena.
- A process paragraphs is related in time order, generally chronological. It usually describes a process or teaches readers how to perform the process.
- Comparing two subjects draws attention to their similarities but can also indicate a consideration of differences. To contrast is to focus only on differences. Both comparisons and contrasts may be examined point-by-point, or in succeeding paragraphs.

Organizing information:

- A grouping of items into categories based on some consistent criteria is called classification. The principle of classification a writer chooses will depend on the purpose of the classification. Most items can be classified by a number of criteria, and the selection of the specific classification will depend on the writer's aims in using this device.
- Division, on the other hand, takes one item and divides it into parts. Just as with classification, the division must be based on a valid and consistent principle. For example a body may be divided into various body systems easily, but not as easily divided into body functions, because the categories overlap.
- Definition classifies a concept or word in a general group, then distinguishes it from other members of the class. Usually simple definitions can be provided in a sentence or two, while more complex ones may need a paragraph or two to adequately define them.

Coherence

A smooth flow of sentences and paragraphs without gaps, shifts, or bumps leads to paragraph coherence. Ties between old information and new, can be smoothed by several strategies.

- Linking ideas clearly, from the topic sentence to the body of the paragraph is essential for a smooth transition. The topic sentence states the main point, and this should be followed by specific details, examples, and illustrations that support the topic sentence. The support may be direct or indirect. In indirect support the illustrations and examples may support a sentence that in turn supports the topic directly.
- The repetition of key words adds coherence to a paragraph. To avoid dull language, variations of the key words may be used.
- Parallel structures are often used within sentences to emphasize the similarity of ideas and connect sentences giving similar information.
- Minimize shifting sentences from one verb tense to another. These shifts affect the smooth flows of words and can disrupt the coherence of the paragraph.

Transitions

Transitions are bridges between what has been read and what is about to be read. Transitions smooth the reader's path between sentences, and inform readers of major connections to new ideas forthcoming in the text. Transitional phrases should be used with care, selecting the appropriate phrase for a transition. Tone is another important consideration in using transitional phrases, varying the tone for different audiences. For example in a scholarly essay, "in summary" would be preferable to the more informal "in short".

When working with transitional words and phrases, writers usually find a natural flow that indicates when a transition is needed. In reading a draft of the text, it should become apparent where the flow is uneven or rough. At this point, the writer can add transitional elements during the revision process. Revising can also afford an opportunity to delete transitional devices that seem heavy-handed or unnecessary.

> **Review Video: Transitions in Writing**
> Visit mometrix.com/academy and enter code: 233246

Lengths of Paragraphs

The comfort level for readers is paragraphs of between 100 and 200 words. Shorter paragraphs cause too much starting and stopping, and give a "choppy" effect. Paragraphs that are too long often test the attention span of the reader. Two notable exceptions to this rule exist. In scientific or scholarly papers, longer paragraphs suggest seriousness and depth. In journalistic writing, constraints are placed on paragraph size by the narrow columns in a newspaper format.

The first and last paragraphs of a text will usually be the introduction and conclusion. These special purpose paragraphs are likely to be shorter than paragraphs in the body of the work. Paragraphs in the body of the essay follow the subject's outline; one paragraph per point in short essays, and a group of paragraphs per point in longer works. Some ideas require more development than others, so it is good for a writer to remain flexible. A too long paragraph may be divided, while shorter ones may be combined.

Paragraph breaks are used for many reasons, usually as devices to improve the flow or content of the text. Some examples for beginning new paragraphs include:

- To mark off the introduction and concluding paragraphs.
- To signal a shift to a new idea or topic.
- To indicate an important shift in time or place.
- To emphasize a point by repositioning a major sentence.
- To highlight a comparison, contrast, or cause and effect relationship.
- To signal a change in speakers, voice, or tense.

Argumentative Writing

Constructing a reasonable argument, the goal is not to "win" or have the last word, but rather to reveal current understanding of the question, and propose a solution to the perceived problem. The purpose of argument in a free society or a research field is to reach the best conclusion possible at the time.

Conventions of arguments vary from culture to culture. In America arguments tend to be direct rather than subtle, carefully organized rather than discursive, spoken plainly rather than poetically. Evidence presented is usually specific and factual, while appeals to intuition or communal wisdom are rare.

Argumentative writing takes a stand on a debatable issue , and seeks to explore all sides of the issue and reach the best possible solution. Argumentative writing should not be combative, at it's strongest it is assertive.

A prelude to argumentative writing is an examination of the issue's social and intellectual contexts.

- 66 -

Introducion

The introduction of an essay arguing an issue should end with a thesis sentence that states a position on the issue. A good strategy is to establish credibility with readers by showing both expert knowledge and fair-mindedness. Building common ground with undecided or neutral readers is helpful.

The thesis should be supported by strong arguments that support the stated position. The main lines of argument should have a cumulative effect of convincing readers that the thesis has merit. The sum of the main lines of argument will outline the overall argumentative essay. The outline will clearly illustrate the central thesis, and subordinate claims that support it.

Evidence must be provided that support both the thesis and supporting arguments. Evidence based on reading should be documented, to show the sources. Readers must know how to check sources for accuracy and validity.

Supporting Evidence

Most arguments must be supported by facts and statistics. Facts are something that is known with certainty, and have been objectively verified. Statistics may be used in selective ways to for partisan purposes. It is good to check statistics by reading authors writing on both sides of an issue. This will give a more accurate idea of how valid are the statistics cited.

Examples and illustrations add an emotional component to arguments, reaching readers in ways that facts and figures cannot. They are most effective when used in combination with objective information that can be verified.

Expert opinion can contribute to a position on a question. The source should be an authority whose credentials are beyond dispute. Sometimes it is necessary to provide the credentials of the expert. Expert testimony can be quoted directly, or may be summarized by the writer. Sources must be well documented to insure their validity.

Counter Arguments

In addition to arguing a position, it is a good practice to review opposing arguments and attempt to counter them. This process can take place anywhere in the essay, but is perhaps best placed after the thesis is stated. Objections can be countered on a point-by-point analysis, or in a summary paragraph. Pointing out flaws in counter arguments is important, as is showing the counter arguments to have less weight than the supported thesis.

Building common ground with neutral or opposed readers can make a strong case. Sharing values with undecided readers can allow people to switch positions without giving up what they feel is important. People who may oppose a position need to feel they can change their minds without compromising their intelligence or their integrity. This appeal to open-mindedness can be a powerful tool in arguing a position without antagonizing opposing views.

Fallacious Arguments

A number of unreasonable argumentative tactics are known as logical fallacies. Most fallacies are misguided uses of legitimate argumentative arguments.

Generalizing is drawing a conclusion from an array of facts using inductive reasoning. These conclusions are a probability, not a certainty. The fallacy known as a "hasty generalization" is a conclusion based on insufficient or unrepresentative evidence. Stereotyping is a hasty generalization about a group. This is common because of the human tendency to perceive selectively. Observations are made through a filter of preconceptions, prejudices, and attitudes.

Analogies point out similarities between disparate things. When an analogy is unreasonable, it is called a "false analogy". This usually consists of assuming if two things are alike in one respect, they must be alike in others. This, of course, may or may not be true. Each comparison must be independently verified to make the argument valid.

Post Hoc Fallacy

Tracing cause and effect can be a complicated matter. Because of the complexity involved, writers often over-simplify it. A common error is to assume that because one event follows another, the first is the cause of the second. This common fallacy is known as "post hoc", from the Latin meaning "after this, therefore because of this".

A post hoc fallacy could run like this: "Since Abner Jones returned to the Giants lineup, the team has much better morale". The fact that Jones returned to the lineup may or may not have had an effect on team morale. The writer must show there is a cause and effect relationship between Jones' return and team morale. It is not enough to note that one event followed another. It must be proved beyond a reasonable doubt that morale was improved by the return of Jones to the lineup. The two may be true but do not necessarily follow a cause and effect pattern.

Assumptions

When considering problems and solutions, the full range of possible options should be mentioned before recommending one solution above others. It is unfair to state there are only two alternatives, when in fact there are more options. Writers who set up a choice between their preferred option and a clearly inferior one are committing the "either...or" fallacy. All reasonable alternatives should be included in the possible solutions.

Assumptions are claims that are taken to be true without proof. If a claim is controversial, proof should be provided to verify the assumption. When a claim is made that few would agree with, the writer is guilty of a "non sequitur" (Latin for "does not follow") fallacy. Thus any assumption that is subject to debate cannot be accepted without supporting evidence is suspect.

Syllogism

Deductive reasoning is constructed in a three-step method called a syllogism. The three steps are the major premise, the minor premise, and the conclusion. The major premise is a generalization, and the minor premise is a specific case. The conclusion is deduced from applying the generalization to the specific case. Deductive arguments fail if either the major or minor premise is not true, or if the conclusion does not logically follow from the premises. This means a deductive argument must stand on valid, verifiable premises, and the conclusion is a logical result of the premises.

"Straw Man" Fallacy

The "straw man" fallacy consists of an oversimplification or distortion of opposing views. This fallacy is one of the most obvious and easily uncovered since it relies on gross distortions. The name comes from a side setting up a position so weak (the straw man) that is easily refuted.

Composition

Composition refers to a range of activities which include the achievement of literacy, transmission of culture, preparation for writing skills in the workplace, and writing as a mode of personal expression and identity. Composition has evolved into an interdisciplinary study and an eclectic practice. Writing is always a process, performing a critical role in education.

Composition studies, like its companion, rhetoric, is a practical and theoretical study Originally it was limited to teaching and correction of student's grammar. Composition has come of age as a writing process, a complex network of interweaving social, political, and individual components.

The field now includes collaborative writing, two or more students writing together, each assuming specific responsibilities with a heavy emphasis on joint revisions. Continued innovations and experimentation are an ongoing part of composition studies.

Literary Devices

Allusions

An allusion is a reference within a text to some person, place, or event outside the text. Allusions that refer to events more or less contemporary with the text are called topical allusions. Those referring to specific persons are called personal allusions. An example of personal allusion is William Butler Yeat's reference to "golden thighed Pythagoras" in his poem " Among School Children".

Allusions may be used to summarize an important idea or point out a contrast between contemporary life and a heroic past. An example of this would be James Joyce's classical parallels in "Ulysses" in which heroic deeds in the "Odyssey" are implicitly compared to the banal aspects of everyday life in Dublin.

Allusions may also be used to summarize an important idea such as the concluding line from "King Kong", "It was beauty killed the beast".

> **Review Video: Allusion**
> Visit mometrix.com/academy and enter code: 294065

Jargon

Jargon is a specialized language used among members of a trade, profession, or group. Jargon should be avoided and used only when the audience will be familiar with the language. Jargon includes exaggerated language usually designed to impress rather than inform. Sentences filled with jargon are both wordy and difficult to understand. Jargon is commonly used in such institutions as the military, politics, sports, and art.

Clichés

Clichés are sentences and phrases that have been overused to the point of triviality. They have no creativity or originality and add very little to modern writing. Writers should avoid clichés whenever possible. When editing writing, the best solution for clichés is to delete them. If this does not seem easily accomplished, a cliché can be modified so that it is not dully predictable and trite. This often means adding phrases or sentences to change the cliché.

Slang

Slang is an informal and sometimes private language that connotes the solidarity and exclusivity of a group such as teenagers, sports fans, ethnic groups, or rock musicians. Slang has a certain vitality, but it is not always widely understood and should be avoided in most writing. An exception could be when the audience is a specialized group who understand the jargon and slang commonly used by the members.

Sexist Language

Sexist language is language that stereotypes or demeans women or men, usually women. Such language is derived from stereotypical thinking, traditional pronoun use, and from words used to refer indefinitely to both sexes. Writers should avoid referring to a profession as being basically male or female, and using different conventions when referring to men and women. Pronouns "he,him,and his"should be avoided by using a pair of pronouns or revising the sentence to obviate the sexist language.

Pretentious Language

In an attempt to sound elegant, profound, poetic, or impressive, some writers embroider their thoughts with flowery phrases, inflated language, and generally pretentious wordage. Pretentious language is often so ornate and wordy that it obscures the true meaning of the writing.

Euphemisms

Euphemisms are pleasant sounding words that replace language that seems overly harsh or ugly. Euphemisms are wordy and indirect, clouding meaning through "pretty" words. However euphemisms are sometimes uses as conventions, when speaking about subjects such as death, bodily functions and sex.

Doublespeak

The term "doublespeak" was coined by George Orwell in his futuristic novel "1984". It applies to any evasive or deceptive language, particularly favored by politicians. Doublespeak is evident in advertising, journalism, and in political polemics. it should be avoided by serious writers.

Figures of Speech

A figure of speech is an expression that uses words imaginatively rather than literally to make abstract ideas concrete. Figures of speech compare unlike things to reveal surprising similarities. The pitfalls of using figures of speech is the failure of writers to think through the images they evoke. The result can be a mixed metaphor, a combination of two or more images that do not make sense together.

In a simile the writer makes an explicit comparison, usually by introducing it with "like" or "as". An example would be " white as a sheet" or "my love is like a red, red, rose". Effective use of similes can add color and vivid imagery to language. Used carefully and sparingly, they provide a writer with an effective device to enhance meaning and style.

Figures of speech are particularly effective when used with discretion and selectively. Examples of figures of speech can be found in all genres of writing.

> **Review Video: Figure of Speech**
> Visit mometrix.com/academy and enter code: 111295

Allegories

Allegories are a type of narrative in which the story reflects at least one other meaning. Traditional allegory often employs personification, the use of human characters to represent abstract ideas. Early examples of the use of allegory were the medieval mystery plays in which abstractions such as Good, Evil, Penance, and Death appeared as characters.

Another type of allegory uses a surface story to refer to historical or political events. Jonathan Swift was a master at using allegory in this manner, particularly in his "Tale of a Tub" (1704), a satirical allegory of the reformation.

Allegory has been largely replaced by symbolism by modern writers. Although they are sometimes confused, symbolism bears a natural relationship to the events in a story, while in allegory the surface story is only an excuse for the secondary and more important meaning. Allegory has had a revival in postmodern writing, and is seen in much contemporary literature.

Ambiguity

In writing historically, ambiguity is generally viewed as an error or flaw. The word now means a literary technique in which a word or phrase conveys two or more different meanings. William Empson defines ambiguity as " any verbal nuance, however slight, which gives room for alternative reactions to the same piece of language." Empons chief purpose in defining ambiguity was to note how this device affects the interpretation of poetry. Empson identified seven types of ambiguity including the traditional meaning. These seven types of ambiguity each provided a different view of possible interpretation of text in writing. Empsons's "Seven Types of Ambiguity" was the first detailed analysis of the phenomena of multiple meanings, sometimes called plurisignation. Ambiguity can be a useful device for some types of writing but does lend itself to informative or persuasive text.

Phonetics

Phonetics seeks to provide a descriptive terminology for the sounds of spoken language. This includes the physiology for the production of speech sounds, the classification of speech sounds including vowels and consonants, the dynamic features of speech production, and the study of instrumental phonetics, the investigation of human speech by laboratory techniques. The dynamic aspects of phonetics include voice quality, stress, rhythm, and speech melody.

Instrumental phonetics underlines both the complexity of speech production, and the subtlety of the human brain in interpreting a constantly changing flow of acoustic data as recognizable speech-sounds. The correlation between acoustic quality, auditory perception, and articulatory position is a complex and not yet fully understood process. It represents a fertile area of research for phoneticians, psychologists, and perhaps philosophers.

General phonetics classifies the speech sounds of all languages. Any one language uses only possibilities of the selections available. Sounds and how they are used in a language is the phonology of a language. Dynamic features of phonology include speech melody, stress, rhythmic organization, length and syllabicity. The central unit of phonology is the phoneme, the smallest distinct sound in a given language. Two words are composed of different phonemes only if they differ phonetically in ways that are found to make a difference in meaning. Phonemic transcription of a word or phrase is its representation as a sequence or other combinations of phonemes.

Phonology

Phonology is a controversial and enigmatic part of linguistics. It is widely studied and defined but there is no agreement on the definition of a phoneme or phonology theory. There may be as many theories as there are phonologies in linguistics.

Linguistics

Linguistics is the branch of knowledge that deals with language. Grammar, an integral part of linguistics, in its widest sense, includes the study of the structure of words and syntactic constructions, and that of sound systems. Linguistics is concerned with the lexical and grammatical categories of individual languages, and the differences between languages and the historical relations between families of languages. Each lexical entry informs us about the linguistic properties of the word. It will indicate a word's phonological, grammatical, and somatic properties.

- Grammar may be said to generate a set of phrases and sentences, so linguistics is also the study of generative grammar. Grammar must also contain a phonological component, since this determines the phonetic form of words in speech.
- Phonology, the study of sound systems and processes affecting the way words are pronounced, is another aspect of linguistics.

Psycholinguistics

Psycholinguistics is concerned with how linguistic competence is employed in the production and comprehension of speech.

- The first step in language comprehension is to use the phonological processor to identify sounds.
- Then the lexical processor identifies the component words.
- Finally the syntactic processor provides a syntactic representation of the sentence.
- The last step is for the semantic processor to compute a meaning representation for the sentence, on the basis of syntactical and lexical information supplied by previous steps in the process.

The relevant meaning of the words serves as the end-product of the process, and once this has been computed the sentence is understood. All stages of the psycholinguistic process take place in real time, so that measurements of each specific part of the process may be compared to the level of complexity of the grammar itself. Such is the experimental study of psycholinguistics applied.

Developmental Linguistics

Neurolinguistics is concerned with the physical representations of linguistic processes in the brain. The most effective way to study this is to observe the effects on language capacity in brain-injured individuals. The frontal lobe of the brain appears to be the area responsible for controlling the production of speech. As research has become more refined over the years, it is evident that language functions are located in different parts of the brain. As improved diagnostic and sophisticated imaging techniques are developed, it is anticipated that the mysteries of language capacity and competence corresponding to specific parts of the brain will become clearer. For now, our knowledge in this field is imperfect, and the process of mapping the brain for linguistic capacity and performance is limited. Neurolinguistics is closely tied to neurology and neuro-physiology.

Sociolinguistics

Sociolinguistics is the study of the relationship between language and the structure of society. It takes into account the social backgrounds of both the speaker and the addressee, the relationship between the speaker and the addressee, and the context and manner of the interaction. Because the emphasis in sociolinguistics is on language use, the analysis of language in this field is typically based on taped recordings of everyday interactions. The sociolinguists seek to discover universal properties of languages, attempting to analyze questions such as "do all languages change in the same ways"? Answers are sought to the larger questions about universals in society in which language plays a major role. The multifaceted nature of language and its broad impact on many areas of society make this field an exciting and cutting edge part of linguistics.

Meaning

Meaning is traditionally something said to be expressed by a sentence. Modern theories in linguistics often elaborate on this. The four major theories are:

1. The meaning of a sentence is different depending on the context of the utterance.
2. Sentence meanings are part of the language system and form a level of semantic representation independent of other levels.
3. Representations are derivable from the level of syntax, given a lexicon which specifies the meaning of words and a set of semantic rules.
4. The meaning of utterances follows from separate principles that are in the domain of context or pragmatics.

Other theories assert that neither words or sentences can be assigned meanings independently of situations in which they are uttered. These theories all seek to establish a standard understanding of meaning so that linguists can refine and extend their research.

Etmology

Etymology is the study of the historical relation between a word and earlier form or forms from which it has developed. Etymology can be loosely defined as the study of the origins of words. This study may occur on different levels of linguistic approach. Word meanings and their historical antecedents are often a complicated and controversial source of study. Tracing the meaning of words often includes understanding the social, political, and cultural time that the definition existed. The evolution of words from earlier forms suggests a cross-fertilization of social contexts and common usage that is a fascinating field of study.

An etymological fallacy is that the notion that a true meaning of a word can be derived from it etymology. Modern linguistic theory provides a substantial body of knowledge that compares and evaluates etymology and provides numerous avenues for new research.

Lexicology

Lexicon is the aspect of a language that is centered on individual words or similar units. Its scope varies widely from one theory to another. In some systems, lexicon is a simple component of generative grammar. In others it is the basis for all grammatical patterns. some view a lexicon as an unstructured list, while others see it as an elaborate network of entries governed by lexical rules and shared features. Lexicon in linguistics is to be distinguished as a theory from a dictionary or part of a practical description.

Lexicology is the branch of linguistics concerned with the semantic structure of the lexicon. Lexical diffusion is the gradual spread of a phonetic or other change across the vocabulary of a language or across a speech community? The term may also refer to the diffusion of individual lexical units within a lexicon.

Lexical decomposition is the analysis of word meanings into smaller units.

Grammar

Grammar may be practically defined as the study of how words are put together or the study of sentences. There are multiple approaches to grammar in modern linguistics. Any systematic account of the structure of a language and the patterns it describes is grammar. Modern definitions of grammar state grammar is the knowledge of a language developed in the minds of the speakers.

A grammar in the broadest sense is a set of rules internalized by members of a speech community, and an account, by a linguist, of such a grammar. This internalized grammar is what is commonly called a language. Grammar is often restricted to units that have meaning. The expanded scope of grammar includes morphology and syntax, and a lexicon. Grammatical meaning is described as part of the syntax and morphology of a language as distinct from its lexicon.

The ability to learn language is determined by a biologically determined innate language facility. This widely accepted theory is known as the innateness hypothesis. The knowledge of adult grammar appears to go far beyond anything supplied by the child's linguistic experience, implying an innate ability to learn language. A language facility must incorporate a set of Universal Grammar principles which enable a child to form and interpret sentences in any natural language. Children have the ability to acquire any natural language so it follows that the contents of the innate language facility must not be specific to any one human language. Developmental linguistics is concerned with examining children's grammar and the conditions under which they emerge. The language faculty is species-specific and the ability to develop a grammar of a language is unique to human beings. The study of non-human communication forms a different field of study.

Structuralized Grammar

Structuralize grammar tends to be formal in nature as it is concerned with grammatical and phonological considerations, rather than semantics. The chief goal is to uncover the structure of a language. There are valid criticisms of the structural approach to grammar. problems exist in the available descriptive frameworks to manage, difficulties with definitions, and inconsistency and contradiction between theory and practice. These concerns have not invalidated the study of structural grammar, but have been utilized by linguists to perfect the analysis.

Transformational Grammar

Transformational grammar is any grammar in which different syntactic structures are related by transformations. The main role of transformations was to relate the sentences of a language as a whole to a small set of kernel sentences. A base component of a grammar generated a deep structure for each sentence. these structures were an input to a transformational component, which was an ordered structure of transformational rules. Its output was a set of surface structures, which combined with the deep structures, formed its syntactic description. Further rules supplied its semantic representation and phonetic representation.

Transformational grammar was invented and promulgated by Noam Chomsky, a revolutionary figure in linguistics. Much of Chomsky's work has been directed to the development of a universal grammar, conceived as an account of what is inherited by the individual. Chomsky remains the dominant figure of the 20th century in linguistics.

Sentences

The largest structural unit normally recognized by grammar is the sentence. Any attempt to accurately define the sentence is in error. Any such definition will not bear up under Linguistic Analysis. In every language, there are a limited number of favorite sentence-types to which most others can be related. They vary from language to language. Certain utterances, while not immediately conforming to favorite sentence types, can be expanded in their context to become one sentence of a particular type. These can be called referable sentences. Other utterances that do not conform to favorite sentence types may reveal obsolete sentence types; these are proverbial sayings and are called gnomic or fossilized sentences. A very small number of utterances not conforming to the favorite sentence-types are found in prescribed social situations, such as "Hello" or "Bye".

Sentence Patterns

Sentence patterns fall into five common modes with some exceptions. They are:

1. Subject / linking verb / subject complement
2. Subject / transitive verb / direct object
3. Subject / transitive verb / indirect object / direct object
4. Subject / transitive verb / direct object / object complement
5. Subject / intransitive verb

Common exceptions to these patterns are questions and commands, sentences with delayed subjects, and passive transformations. Writers sometimes use the passive voice when the active voice would be more appropriate.

Sentences Classification

Sentences are classified in two ways:

1. according to their structure
2. according to their purpose

Writers use declarative sentences to make statements, imperative sentences to issue requests or commands, interrogative sentences to ask questions, and exclamatory sentences to make exclamations.

Depending on the number and types of clauses they contain, sentences may be classified as simple, compound, complex, or compound-complex.

Clauses come in two varieties: independent and subordinate.

1. An independent clause is a full sentence pattern that does not function within another sentence pattern; it contains a subject and modifiers plus a verb and any objects, complements, and modifiers of that verb. It either stands alone or could stand alone.
2. A subordinate clause is a full sentence pattern that functions within a sentence as an adjective, an adverb, or a noun but that cannot stand alone as a complete sentence.

Sentence Structures

The four major types of sentence structure are:

1. Simple sentences - Simple sentences have one independent clause with no subordinate clauses. a simple sentence may contain compound elements,- a compound subject, verb, or object for example, but does not contain more than one full sentence pattern.
2. Compound sentences - Compound sentences are composed of two or more independent clauses with no subordinate clauses. The independent clauses are usually joined with a comma and a coordinating conjunction, or with a semicolon.

3. Complex sentences - A complex sentence is composed of one independent clause with one or more dependent clauses.
4. Compound-complex sentences - A compound-complex sentence contains at least two independent clauses and at least one subordinate clause. sometimes they contain two full sentence patters that can stand alone. When each independent clause contains a subordinate clause, this makes the sentence both compound and complex.

> **Review Video: Sentence Structure**
> Visit mometrix.com/academy and enter code: 700478

Chomsky's Sentence Structure

Deep structure is a representation of the syntax of a sentence distinguished by various criteria from its surface structure. Initially defined by Noam Chomsky as the part of the syntactic description of a of a sentence that determines its semantic interpretation by the base component of a generative grammar.

Surface sentence structure is a representation of the syntax of a sentence seen as deriving by one ore more transformations, from a an underlying deep structure. Such a sentence is in the order in which the corresponding phonetic forms are spoken. Surface structure was later broadened by Chomsky to include semantic structure. Chomsky's later minimalist program no longer takes this for granted. Minimalist theory assumes no more than a minimum of types of statements and levels of representation.

The technical analysis outlined by Chomsky over three decades forms an integral part of transformational grammar.

Language Investigation

The investigation of a language by classification is the goal of the modern linguist. When the observer has determined the phonemic structure of a language, and has classified all its constructions, both morphological and syntactic, the resulting description will be an accurate and usable grammar of the language, accounting in the simplest way for all the utterances of the speech community.

Language Families

A language family is a group of languages that have been developed from a single ancestor. An example would be Indo-European, of which English is one of many members. Language families are identified whenever a common origin can be accepted as certain. When a family origin in speculative or uncertain, it may be called a projected family, a proposed family, or a probable family.

Some linguists have tried to apply a biological method of classification of language families, following the genus, order, species model. They have classed languages as beginning with "superficies", "macro families", "stocks", "super stocks", or "phyla" at the top. Below those will be "subfamilies", "branches", and "groups". This attempt has proved faulty as the classifications imply more than is known about family origins. It has been difficult and largely unaccepted to class language families in these descending modes of importance.

Language Descriptions

The levels of language descriptions represent a distinct phase in the description of a language at which specific types of elements and the relations between them are studied or investigated.

- At the level of phonology, one studies the sound structure of a language, words or larger units that are specific to that level.
- At the level of syntax, sentences are represented as the configuration of words or morphemes standing in specific construction in relationship to one another.

Levels of language are an important part of structural linguistics, whether they focus on formal analyses or representation. Some give an order of procedures which govern the formal structural analysis of language. Others propose a hierarchy of greater or lesser degrees of abstraction, ranging from phonetics as the highest and semantics as the lowest. In many of these levels are defined by the different components of an integrated structural grammar.

Morphology

Morphology is the grammatical structure of words and their categories. The morphological process includes any of the formal processes or operations by which the forms of words are derived from stems or roots. Types of morphological processes include affix, any element in the structure of a word other than a root; reduplication, where all or part of a form is duplicated; subtraction, where part of a form is deleted; supple ton, where one part of the morphological process replaces another; compound, where two parts of the morphological process are joined; and modification, where one part of a form is modified.

Forms of morphological classification distinguished isolating, in which each grammatical classification is represented by a single word, agglutinating, where words are easily divided into separate sections, and inflectional, concerned with inflections in languages.

Functions of Language

- Language is a means of social control making human society possible. The communication of thoughts is but a small part of this.
- Language acts as an index to various things about the speaker - age, sex, physical and mental wellbeing, and personality characteristics.
- Language acts to limit classes within a society, either by accent, dialect, choice of words and grammatical features.
- Language brings human beings into relationship with the external world. It mediates between man and his environment.
- Language is the material of artistic creation, including not only literary works but poetic and oral traditions.

Any list of languages functions is arbitrary. There are dozens of other possible classifications of language functions in the literature of linguistics. The classification given above includes the basic elements of language and their societal effect.

Semantics

Semantics studies the meaning of utterances and why particular utterances have the meanings they do. Semantics originally covered grammar, the account of meaningful forms, and the lexicon or body of words contained in a language. When the study of forms was separated from that of meanings, the field of generative grammar became associated with semantics. Currently, the scope of semantics will cover word meanings or lexical semantics, and the meaning of utterances studied in pragmatics, the meaning of language in everyday life.

Some narrow definitions of semantics understand the term to mean the study of problems encounted in formal semantics, excluding lexical meaning completely. This last definition is an extreme one, and is included to illustrate the broad vistas that are opened when we discuss semantics. What can be asserted is that semantics in its broadest and most common usage is the field of study in linguistics that deals with meaning in all its forms.

Spoken and Written Language

The relationship of spoken language and written form has been the subject of differences of attitudes among linguists. The spoken form is historically prior, both for the language community and the individual. It is also more complicated. For these reasons, emphasis is placed on the sound systems of languages which has led some linguists to describe the spoken form as language, and the written form as written language. Both are equal examples of language. The relationship is not a straightforward case of deriving the written from the spoken form. When a written form evolves, it tends to take on a life of its own and acquires usages different from the spoken.

Linguists are concerned with the analysis and development of language as a whole, both written and spoken. Much of the controversy in linguistic theory is concerned with both forms of languages. Linguistics is in a sense a search for the universals in language, which includes both spoken and written forms.

Parts of Speech

Nouns

Nouns are the name of a person, place, or thing, and are usually signaled by an article (a, an, the). Nouns sometimes function as adjectives modifying other nouns. Nouns used in this manner are called noun/adjectives. Nouns are classified for a number of purposes: capitalization, word choice, count/no count nouns, and collective nouns are examples.

Pronouns

Pronouns is a word used in place of a noun. Usually the pronoun substitutes for the specific noun, called the antecedent. Although most pronouns function as substitutes for nouns, some can function as adjectives modifying nouns. pronouns may be classed as personal, possessive, intensive, relative, interrogative, demonstrative, indefinite, and reciprocal. pronouns can cause a number of problems for writers including pronoun-antecedent agreement, distinguishing between who and whom, and differentiating pronouns such as I and me.

Problems with Pronouns

Pronouns are words that substitute for nouns: he, it, them, her, me, and so on. Four frequently encountered problems with pronouns include:

1. Pronoun - antecedent agreement - The antecedent of a pronoun is the word the pronoun refers to. A pronoun and its antecedent agree when they are both singular or plural.
2. Pronoun reference - A pronoun should refer clearly to its antecedent. A pronoun's reference will be unclear if it id ambiguous, implied, vague, or indefinite.

3. Personal pronouns - Some pronouns change their case form according to their grammatical structure in a sentence. Pronouns functioning as subjects appear in the subjective case, those functioning as objects appear in the objective case, and those functioning as possessives appear in the possessive case.

4. Who or whom - Who, a subjective-case pronoun, can only be used subjects and subject complements. Whom, an objective case pronoun, can only be used for objects. The words who and whom appear primarily in subordinate clauses or in questions.

Review Video: <u>Nouns and Pronouns</u>
Visit mometrix.com/academy and enter code: 312073

Verbs

The verb of a sentence usually expresses action or being. It is composed of a main verb and sometimes supporting verbs. These helping verbs are forms of have, do, and be, and nine modals. The modals are "can, could, may, might, shall, should, will, would, and ought". Some verbs are followed by words that look like prepositions, but are so closely associated with the verb to be part of its meaning. These words are known as particles, and examples include "call off", "look up", and "drop off".

The main verb of a sentence is always one that would change form from base form to past tense, past participle, present participle and, -s forms. When both the past-tense and past-participle forms of a verb end in "ed", the verb is regular. In all other cases the verb is irregular. The verb "be" is highly irregular, having eight forms instead of the usual five.

- Linking verbs link the subject to a subject complement, a word or word group that completes the meaning of the subject by renaming or describing it.
- A transitive verb takes a direct object, a word or word group that names a receiver of the action. The direct object of a transitive verb is sometimes preceded by an indirect object. Transitive verbs usually appear in the active voice, with a subject doing the action and a direct object receiving the action. The direct object of a transitive verb is sometimes followed by an object complement, a word or word group that completes the direct object's meaning by renaming or describing it.
- Intransitive verbs take no objects or complements. Their pattern is subject verb.

A dictionary will disclose whether a verb is transitive or intransitive. Some verbs have both transitive and intransitive functions.

Verb Phrases

A verbal phrase is a verb form that does not function as the verb of a clause. There are three major types of verbal phrases:

1. Participial phrases - These always function as adjectives. Their verbals are always present participles, always ending in "ing", or past participles frequently ending in "-d,-ed,-n.-en,or -t". Participial phrases frequently appear immediately following the noun or pronoun they modify.

2. Gerund phrases - Gerund phrases are built around present participles and they always function as nouns. : usually as subjects subject complements, direct objects, or objects of a preposition.

3. Infinitive phrases are usually structured around "to" plus the base form of the verb. They can function as nouns, as adjectives, or as adverbs. When functioning as a noun, an infinitive phrase may appear in almost any noun slot in a sentence, usually as a subject, subject complement, or direct object. Infinitive phrases functioning as adjectives usually appear immediately following the noun or pronoun they modify. adverbial phrases usually qualify the meaning of the verb.

Problems with Verbs

The verb is the heart of the sentence. Verbs have several potential problems including:

- Irregular verbs - Verbs that do not follow usual grammatical rules.
- Tense - Tenses indicate the time of an action in relation to the time of speaking or writing about the action.
- Mood - There are three moods in English: the indicative, used for facts, opinions, and questions; the imperative, used for orders or advice, and the subjunctive, used for wishes. The subjective mood is the most likely to cause problems. The subjective mood is used for wishes, and in "if"clauses expressing conditions contrary to facts. The subjective in such cases is the past tense form of the verb; in the case of "be", it is always "were", even if the subject is singular. The subjective mood is also used in "that' clauses following verbs such as "ask, insist, recommend, and request. The subjunctive in such cases is the base or dictionary form of the verb.

Adjectives

An adjective is a word use to modify or describe a noun or pronoun. An adjective usually answers one of these question: "Which one?, What kind of?, and How many?" Adjectives usually precede the words they modify, although they sometimes follow linking verbs, in which case they describe the subject. Most adjectives have three forms: the positive, the comparative, and the superlative. The comparative should be used to compare two things, the superlative to compare three or more things.

> **Review Video: What is an Adjective?**
> Visit mometrix.com/academy and enter code: 470154

Articles

Articles, sometimes classed as adjectives, are used to mark nouns. There are only three: the definite article "the" and the indefinite articles "a" and "an."

Adverbs

An adverb is a word used to modify or qualify a verb, adjective, or another adverb. It usually answers one of these questions: "When?, where?, how?, and why?" Adverbs modifying adjectives or other adverbs usually intensify or limit the intensity of words they modify. The negators "not" and "never" are classified as adverbs. Writers sometimes misuse adverbs, and multilingual speakers have trouble placing them correctly. Most adverbs also have three forms: the positive, the comparative, and the superlative. The comparative should be used to compare two things, the superlative to compare three or more things.

> **Review Video: Adverbs**
> Visit mometrix.com/academy and enter code: 713951

Prepositions

A preposition is a word placed before a noun or pronoun to form a phrase modifying another word in the sentence. The prepositional phrase usually functions as an adjective or adverb. There are a limited number of prepositions in English, perhaps around 80. Some prepositions are more than one word long. "Along with", "listen to", and "next to" are some examples.

> **Review Video: What is a Preposition?**
> Visit mometrix.com/academy and enter code: 946763

Conjunctions

Conjunctions join words, phrases, or clauses, and they indicate the relationship between the elements that are joined. There are coordinating conjunctions that connect grammatically equal element, correlative conjunctions that connect pairs, subordinating conjunctions that introduces a subordinate clause, and conjunctive adverbs which may be used with a semicolon to connect independent clauses. The most common conjunctive adverbs include "then, thus, and however". Using adverbs correctly helps avoid sentence fragments and run-on sentences.

> **Review Video: Coordinating and Correlative Conjunctions**
> Visit mometrix.com/academy and enter code: 390329
>
> **Review Video: Subordinating Conjunctions**
> Visit mometrix.com/academy and enter code: 958913

Subjects

The subject of a sentence names who or what the sentence is about. The complete subject is composed of the simple subject and all of its modifiers.

To find the complete subject, ask "Who" or "What", and insert the verb to complete the question. The answer is the complete subject. To find the simple subject, strip away all the modifiers in the complete subject.

In imperative sentences, the verb's subject is understood but not actually present in the sentence. Although the subject ordinarily comes before the verb, sentences that begin with "There are" or "There was", the subject follows the verb.

The ability to recognize the subject of a sentence helps in editing a variety of problems such as sentence fragments and subject-verb agreement, as well as the choice of pronouns.

> **Review Video: Subjects**
> Visit mometrix.com/academy and enter code: 444771

Subordinate Word Groups

Subordinate word groups cannot stand alone. They function only within sentences, as adjectives, adverbs, or nouns.

- Prepositional phrases begins with a preposition and ends with a noun or noun equivalent called its object. Prepositional phrases function as adjectives or adverbs.
- Subordinate clauses are patterned like sentences, having subject, verbs, and objects or complements. They function within sentences as adverbs, adjectives, or nouns.

- Adjective clauses modify nouns or pronouns and begin with a relative pronoun or relative adverb.
- Adverb clauses modify verbs, adjectives, and other adverbs.
- Noun clauses function as subjects, objects, or complements. In both adjective and noun clauses words may appear out of their normal order. The parts of a noun clause may also appear in their normal order.

Appositive and Absolute Phrases

Strictly speaking, appositive phrases are not subordinate word groups. Appositive phrases function somewhat as adjectives do, to describe nouns or pronouns. Instead of modifying nouns or pronouns however, appositive phrases rename them. In form they are nouns or nouns equivalents. Appositives are said to be in " in apposition" to the nouns or pronouns they rename. For example, in the sentence "Terriers, hunters at heart, have been dandled up to look like lap dogs", "hunters at heart" is apposition to the noun "terriers".

An absolute phrase modifies a whole clause or sentence, not just one word, and it may appear nearly anywhere in the sentence. It consists of a noun or noun equivalent usually followed by a participial phrase. Both appositive and absolute phrases can cause confusion in their usage in grammatical structures. They are particularly difficult for a person whose first language is not English.

Common Problems with Sentences

Subject-Verb Agreement

In the present tense, verbs agree with their subjects in number, (singular or plural), and in person, (first ,second, or third). The present tense ending -s is used on a verb if its subject is third person singular; otherwise the verb takes no ending. The verb "be" varies from this pattern, and alone among verbs it has special forms in both the present and past tense.

Problems with subject-verb agreement tend to arise in certain contexts:

- Words between subject and verbs.
- Subjects joined by "and".
- Subjects joined by "or" or "nor".
- Indefinite pronouns such as "someone".
- Collective nouns.
- Subject after verb.
- Who, which, and that.
- Plural form, singular meaning.
- Titles, company names, and words mentioned as words.

> **Review Video:** Subject Verb Agreement
> Visit mometrix.com/academy and enter code: 479190

Sentence Fragments

As a rule a part of a sentence should not be treated as a complete sentence. A sentence must be composed of at least one full independent clause. An independent clause has a subject, a verb, and can stand alone as a sentence. Some fragments are clauses that contain a subject and a verb, but begin with a subordinating word. Other fragments lack a subject, verb, or both.

A sentence fragment can be repaired by combining the fragment with a nearby sentence, punctuating the new sentence correctly, or turn the fragment into a sentence by adding the missing elements. Some sentence fragments are used by writers for emphasis. Although sentence fragments are sometimes acceptable, readers and writers do not always agree on when they are appropriate. A conservative approach is to write in complete sentences only unless a special circumstance dictates otherwise.

Run-On Sentences

Run-on sentences are independent clauses that have not been joined correctly. An independent clause is a word group that does or could stand alone in a sentence. When two or more independent clauses appear in one sentence, they must be joined in one of these ways:

- Revision with a comma and a coordinating conjunction.
- Revision with a semicolon, a colon, or a dash. Used when independent clauses are closely related and their relationship is clear without a coordinating conjunction.
- Revision by separating sentences. This approach may be used when both independent clauses are long,
- or if one is a question and one is not. Separate sentences may be the best option in this case.
- Revision by restructuring the sentence. For sentence variety, consider restructuring the sentence, perhaps by turning one of the independent clauses into a subordinate phrase or clause.

Usually one of these choices will be an obvious solution to the run-on sentence. The fourth technique above is often the most effective solution, but requires the most revision.

> **Review Video:** Fragments and Run-on Sentences
> Visit mometrix.com/academy and enter code: 541989

Double Negatives

Standard English allows two negatives only if a positive meaning is intended. "The team was not displeased with their performance" is an example. Double negatives used to emphasize negation are nonstandard.

Negative modifiers such as "never, no, and not" should not be paired with other negative modifiers or negative words such as " none, nobody, nothing, or neither". The modifiers "hardly, barely, and scarcely" are also considered negatives in standard English, so they should not be used with other negatives such as "not, no one, or never".

Double Superlatives

Do not use double superlatives or comparatives. When "er" or "est" has been added to an adjective or adverb, avoid using "more" or "most". Avoid expressions such as "more perfect", and "very round". Either something is or is not. It is not logical to suggest that absolute concepts come in degrees. Use the comparative to compare two things, and the superlative to compare three or more things.

Punctuation

Commas

The comma was invented to help readers. Without it, sentence parts can run together, making meanings unclear. Various rules for comma use include:

- Use a comma before a coordinating conjunction joining independent clauses.
- Use a comma after an introductory clause or phrase.
- Use a comma between items in a series.
- Use a comma between coordinate adjectives not joined with "and". Do not use a comma between cumulative adjectives.
- Use commas to set off nonrestrictive elements. Do not use commas to set off restrictive elements.
- Use commas to set off transitional and parenthetical expressions, absolute phrases, and elements expressing contrast.
- Use commas to set off nouns of direct address, the words yes and no, interrogative tags, and interjections.
- Use commas with dates, addresses, titles, and numbers.

Some situations where commas are unnecessary include:

- Do not use a comma between compound elements that are not independent clauses.
- Do not use a comma after a phrase that begins with an inverted sentence.
- Do not use a comma between the first or after the last item in a series or before the word "although".
- Do not use a comma between cumulative adjectives, between an adjective and a noun, or between an adverb and an adjective.
- Do not use commas to set off restrictive or mildly parenthetical elements or to set off an indirect quotation.
- Do not use a comma to set off a concluding adverb clause that is essential to the meaning of the sentence or after the word "although".
- Do not use a comma to separate a verb from its subject or object. Do not use a comma after a coordinating conjunction or before a parenthesis.
- Do not use a comma with a question mark or an exclamation point.
- Use commas to prevent confusion.
- Use commas to set off direct quotations.

> **Review Video: Commas**
> Visit mometrix.com/academy and enter code: 786797

Semicolons

The semicolon is used to connect major sentence elements of equal grammatical rank. Some rules regarding semicolons include:

- Use a semicolon between closely related independent clauses not joined with a coordinating conjunction.
- Use a semicolon between independent clauses linked with a transitional expression.
- Use a semicolon between items in a series containing internal punctuation.
- Avoid using a semicolon between a subordinate clause and the rest of the sentence.

- Avoid using a semicolon between an appositive word and the word it refers to.
- Avoid using a semicolon to introduce a list.
- Avoid using a semicolon between independent clauses joined by "and, but, or, nor, for, so, or yet".

Review Video: Semicolon Usage
Visit mometrix.com/academy and enter code: 370605

Colons

The colon is used primarily to call attention to the words that follow it. In addition the colon has some other conventional uses:

- Use a colon after an independent clause to direct attention to a list, an appositive, or a quotation.
- Use a colon between independent clauses if the second summarizes or explains the first.
- Use a colon after the salutation in a formal letter, to indicate hours and minutes, to show proportions between a title and subtitle, and between city and publisher in bibliographic entries.

A colon must be preceded by a full independent clause. Avoid using colons in the following situations:

- Avoid using a colon between a verb and its object or complement.
- Avoid using a colon between a preposition and its object.
- Avoid using a colon after "such as, including, or for example."

Apostrophes

An apostrophe is used to indicate that a noun is possessive. Possessive nouns usually indicate ownership, as in Bill's coat or the dog's biscuit. Sometimes ownership is only loosely implied, as in the dog's coat or the forest's trees. If it is unclear whether a noun is possessive, turning into phrase may clarify it.

If the noun is plural and ends in-s, add only an apostrophe. To show joint possession, use -'s with the last noun only. To show individual possession, make all nouns possessive.

An apostrophe is often optional in plural numbers, letters, abbreviations, and words mentioned as words.

Common errors in using apostrophes include:

- Do not use an apostrophe with nouns that are not possessive.
- Do not use an apostrophe in the possessive pronouns "its, whose, his, hers, ours, yours, and theirs".

Review Video: Apostrophes
Visit mometrix.com/academy and enter code: 213068

Quotation Marks

Use quotation marks to enclose direct quotations of a person's words, spoken or written. Do not use quotation marks around indirect quotations. An indirect quotation reports someone's ideas without using that person's exact words.

Set off long quotations of prose or poetry by indenting. Use single quotation marks to enclose a quotation within a quotation. Quotation marks should be used around the titles of short works: newspaper and magazine articles, poems, short stories, songs, episodes of television and radio programs, and subdivisions of books or web sites.

Quotation marks may be used to set off words used as words. Punctuation is used with quotation marks according to convention. Periods and commas are placed inside quotation marks, while colons and semicolons are placed outside quotation marks. Question marks and exclamation points are placed inside quotation marks.

Do not use quotation marks around the title of your own essay.

> **Review Video: Quotation Marks**
> Visit mometrix.com/academy and enter code: 884918

Dashes

When typing, use two hyphens to form a dash. Do not put spaces before or after the dash. Dashes are used for the following purposes:

- To set off parenthetical material that deserves emphasis.
- To set off appositives that contain commas.
- To prepare for a list, a restatement, an amplification, or a dramatic shift in tone or thought.

Unless there is a specific reason for using the dash, omit it. It can give text a choppy effect.

Parentheses

Parentheses are used to enclose supplemental material, minor digressions, and afterthoughts. They are also used to enclose letters or numbers labeling them items in a series. Parentheses should be used sparingly, as they break up text in a distracting manner when overused.

Brackets

Brackets are used to enclose any words or phrases that have been inserted into an otherwise word-for-word quotation.

Ellipsis Marks

The ellipsis mark consists of three spaced periods (...), and is used to indicate when certain words have been deleted from an otherwise word-for-word quotation. If a full sentence or more is deleted in the middle of quoted passage, a person should be inserted before the ellipsis dots. The ellipsis mark should not be used at the beginning of a quotation. It should also not be used at the end of a quotation unless some words have been deleted from the end of the final sentence.

Slashes

The slash, (/), may be used to separate two or three lines of poetry that have been run into a text. If there are more than three lines of poetry they should be handled as an indented quotation. The slash may occasionally be used to separate paired terms such as passed/failed or either/or. In this case, apace is not placed before or after the slash. The slash should be used sparingly, only when it is clearly appropriate.

<u>End Punctuations</u>

- Use a period to end all sentences except direct questions or genuine exclamations. Periods should be used in abbreviations according to convention. Problems can arise when there is a choice between a period and a question mark or exclamation point. If a sentence reports a question rather than asking it directly, it should end with a period, not a question mark.
- Question marks should be used following a direct question. If a polite request is written in the form of a question, it may be followed by a period. Questions in a series may be followed by question marks even when they are not in complete sentences.
- Exclamation marks are used after a word group or sentence that expresses exceptional feeling or deserves special emphasis. Exclamation marks should not be overused, being reserved for appropriate exclamatory interjections.

Essays

Essays are generally defined to describe a prose composition, relatively brief (rarely exceeding 25 pages), dealing with a specific topic. Originally, essays tended to be informal in tone and exploratory and tentative in approach and conclusions. In more modern writing, essays have divided into the formal and informal. The formal essays have dominated the professional and scientific fields, while the informal style is written primarily to entertain or give opinions. Writers should be mindful of the style of essay their subject lends itself to, and conform to the conventions of that style.

Some types of essays, particularly scientific and academic writing, have style manuals to guide the format and conventions of the writing. The Modern Language Association and the American Psychological Association have two of the most widely followed style manuals. They are widely available for writers' reference.

Virginia Practice Test

Writing

1. Which of the following sentences has the modifier correctly placed?

    a. The ripped boy's jeans were muddy and wet.
    b. The hot mug was placed on the coffee table.
    c. The smashed girl's pumpkin lay at the bottom of the stairs.
    d. She only paid $45.00 for her concert ticket.

2. Which of the following sentences does **not** correctly place the modifier?

    a. I found a gold ring walking home.
    b. I slowly sipped the water.
    c. She returned the stained shirt to the store.
    d. Watching the fireworks, the child was mesmerized by the colors.

3. Choose the word that uses parallel structure to complete the sentence.

Chase watered the flowers, mowed the lawn, and _____ the pool.

    a. was vacuuming
    b. vacuumed
    c. he vacuumed
    d. vacuums

4. Choose the word that does **not** establish parallelism with the other answer choices.

    a. hiking
    b. swimming
    c. ran
    d. eating

5. Which of the following sentences does **not** use parallel sentence structure?

    a. Jose wants to return the item and spoke to a manager.
    b. The wall was spackled, sanded, and painted.
    c. She looked forward to picking, scooping, and carving the pumpkin.
    d. They visited the museum, the theater, and the Statue of Liberty.

6. Choose the option that contains a fragment.

    a. Thanksgiving always falls on a Thursday, which leads into Black Friday. Many people stay up all night.
    b. George practiced his multiplication facts every night for a week. Still, he failed the test.
    c. Jessie dreamed of owning a stable and raising horses. She knew exactly which horse would be her first purchase. The large horse with a beautiful mane.
    d. The castle was built on a hill to maintain privacy and intrigue.

7. Which of the following contains a comma splice?

    a. Many athletes have personal trainers, trainers help them stay fit in the off-season.
    b. The child didn't finish his dinner, so his mother would not allow him to have dessert.
    c. We were able to attend the dinner; however, we were not able to attend the after-party.
    d. Tom enjoys fiction, while Jack prefers autobiographies.

8. Identify the run-on sentence.

    a. We loved climbing the mountain and enjoying the beautiful view.
    b. Jonathan lived in Utah, but now he lives in Nebraska with his entire extended family.
    c. I learned what marine biologists do I think I would like to pursue that career.
    d. She is beautiful, but her manners are atrocious.

9. Which of the following contains an error in syntax?

    a. Regardless, he purchased the wine.
    b. Her foul mouth proved that she lacked manners.
    c. She wanted to ensure a reservation at the restaurant.
    d. For all intensive purposes, the book was discontinued.

10. "Do pigs fly?" is an example of which type of writing?

    a. descriptive
    b. rhetorical
    c. sequential
    d. expository

11. "The professor said on Monday she would return our papers" contains which of the following errors?

    a. spelling
    b. misplaced modifier
    c. capitalization
    d. comma splice

12. "The forecast called for rain, so James packed his umbrella" is an example of which type of organizational writing?

    a. compare and contrast
    b. sequential
    c. spatial
    d. problem and solution

13. "We adopted a dog. A giant Rhodesian Ridgeback." This contains _____.

    a. a fragment
    b. a capitalization error
    c. an error in word usage
    d. a spelling error

14. Determine the meaning of the underlined word.

The hikers immediately fed the <u>emaciated</u> dog.

    a. vicious
    b. abnormally thin
    c. withdrawn
    d. missing

15. Identify the synonym for the underlined word.

Stacey <u>abhorred</u> cooking, but loved to eat.

    a. enjoyed
    b. laborious
    c. cuisine
    d. detested

16. Identify the synonym for the underlined word.

Fiona's smirk showed her <u>content</u> with the outcome of the election.

    a. subject matter
    b. disapproval
    c. satisfaction
    d. condemnation

17. Identify the word that best completes the sentence.

The football player blasted _____ the defense and scored his first touchdown.

    a. threw
    b. through
    c. passed
    d. huddled

18. Choose the word that best completes the sentence.

Brody scored more baskets _____ Hank.

    a. then
    b. than
    c. thin
    d. above

19. Choose the word that best completes the sentence.

_____ going to wash the dishes after they clear the table.

    a. There
    b. Their
    c. They're
    d. We'll

20. Choose the word that best completes the sentence.

Her excellent _____ allowed her to read the billboard from a long distance.

    a. site
    b. cite
    c. hearing
    d. vision

21. Choose the word that best completes the sentence.

Based on his decision to flee, the jury _____ that he was guilty.

    a. implied
    b. inferred
    c. loathed
    d. gloated

22. Choose the word or phrase that best completes the sentence.

The flood insurance was expensive, but it offered the homeowner _____ during the hurricane.

  a. piece of mind
  b. luxury
  c. reassurance
  d. apprehension

23. When speaking with fellow electricians about a new project, Gus is most likely to speak in which form of diction?

  a. slang
  b. jargon
  c. colloquial
  d. abstract

24. Tone is used to _____.

  a. show the meaning of an unknown word.
  b. convey the attitude of an author or character.
  c. determine an appropriate pronoun.
  d. determine an author's organizational style.

25. Which of the following best describes the tone of the author?

As he fidgeted with his keys, his knees trembled and his voice quivered. He couldn't find the words to explain how he ended up there.

  a. anxious
  b. excited
  c. foolish
  d. depressed

26. Choose the word or phrase that best completes the sentence.

The woman often _____ before work.

  a. jogs
  b. jogging
  c. have jogged
  d. been jogging

27. Choose the word or phrase that best completes the sentence.

Sadly, Robert _____ homeless for nearly two years.

  a. been
  b. is being
  c. is
  d. has been

28. Select the word or phrase that corrects an error in the underlined portion of the text. If no correction is needed, select "no correction needed."

The leopard gecko is the gecko most often kept as a pet. It is nocturnal and <u>had</u> different color variations.

    a. depicted
    b. has
    c. showed
    d. no correction needed

29. Select the word or phrase that corrects an error in the underlined portion of the text. If no correction is needed, select "no correction needed."

In 2010, an oil spill occurred in the Gulf of Mexico. Today, the effects of that spill still <u>alter</u> the nesting habits of pelicans native to the area.

    a. altered
    b. altering
    c. have altered
    d. no correction needed

30. Select the word or phrase that corrects an error in the underlined portion of the text. If no correction is needed, select "no correction needed."

In 2016, thousands protested the Dakota Access Oil Pipeline. These protestors included over 2,000 veterans, who <u>gather</u> to show their outrage.

    a. were gathering
    b. gathers
    c. gathered
    d. no correction needed

31. Choose the verb that correctly completes the sentence.

At night, the three wolves _____ at the moon.

    a. howl
    b. howls
    c. howling
    d. barking

32. Choose the verb that correctly completes the sentence.

Neither my brother nor my sister is able to _____ the graduation.

    a. attending
    b. attends
    c. attended
    d. attend

33. Select the word or phrase that corrects an error in one of the underlined portions of the text. If no correction is needed, select "no correction needed."

Mayor Williams, <u>whose</u> eyes bulged out of his head, stared at <u>his</u> watch in anticipation.

    a. who's
    b. its
    c. it's
    d. no correction needed

34. Select the word or phrase that corrects an error in the underlined portion of the text. If no correction is needed, select "no correction needed."

The end of the rainbow seemed to touch the ground, luring spectators toward <u>it's</u> promised treasure.

    a. his
    b. its
    c. their
    d. no correction needed

35. Select the word or phrase that corrects an error in the underlined portion of the text.

If you complete your assignments and study for your exams, <u>most</u> will ace the class.

    a. we
    b. they
    c. you
    d. us

36. Select the word or phrase that corrects an error in one of the underlined portions of the text. If no correction is needed, select "no correction needed."

When we asked the waitress for more bread, we were told that <u>you</u> are only <u>allowed</u> one basket per table.

    a. allowing
    b. allows
    c. we
    d. no correction needed

37. Identify the grammatical error illustrated in the sentence.

Ana told Kristen that their principal suspects her of falsifying grades.

    a. spelling
    b. punctuation
    c. capitalization
    d. pronoun

38. Choose the pronoun that best completes the sentence.

The dog _____ my roommate rescued is quickly adjusting to life in the city.

    a. who
    b. that
    c. whom
    d. when

39. In the sentence, "They followed the car to an abandoned lot" the pronoun can best be described as _____.

    a. subjective
    b. objective
    c. possessive
    d. ambiguous

40. In the question, "Where did you find her shoe?" the pronoun "her" can best be described as _____.

    a. subjective
    b. objective
    c. possessive
    d. ambiguous

41. Identify the error in the following sentence: "He ran quick."

    a. misplaced modifier
    b. ambiguous pronoun
    c. adjective/adverb confusion
    d. antecedent confusion

42. Identify the part of speech for the underlined word.

What a <u>lively</u> concert!

    a. verb
    b. adjective
    c. adverb
    d. pronoun

43. Choose the word that best completes the sentence.

The first apple of the season always tastes the _____.

    a. juicy
    b. juicier
    c. juiciest
    d. juiced

44. Choose the word that best completes the sentence.

An elephant is _____ than a mouse.

    a. heavy
    b. heavier
    c. heaviest
    d. biggest

45. Select the word or phrase that corrects an error in one of the underlined portions of the text. If no correction is needed, select "no correction needed."

"I am <u>definately</u> sleeping in <u>tomorrow</u>."

    a. definitely
    b. tommorrow
    c. tomorow
    d. no correction needed

46. Select the word or phrase that corrects an error in the underlined portion of the text. If no correction is needed, select "no correction needed."

The game was <u>canceled</u> and removed from the <u>calendar</u>.

    a. cancilled
    b. calender
    c. calandar
    d. no correction needed

47. Identify the correction needed in the sentence.

"The season finale is fast approaching; and I still don't know which singer I'm rooting for."

    a. add a hyphen: "fast-approaching"
    b. omit the semicolon
    c. "rooting" should be "routing"
    d. the period should be replaced with a question mark

48. Identify the correction needed in the sentence.

The lotion worked so well, it left my skin feeling like a childs.

    a. "worked" should be "work"
    b. omit the comma
    c. "feeling" should be "feel"
    d. "childs" should be "child's"

49. Select the word or phrase that corrects an error in one of the underlined portions of the text. If no correction is needed, select "no correction needed."

The <u>Museum</u> of Natural History has a new <u>dinosaur</u>, the <u>titanosaur</u>.

    a. museum
    b. Dinosaur
    c. Titanosaur
    d. no correction needed

50. Select the word or phrase that corrects an error in one of the underlined portions of the text. If no correction is needed, select "no correction needed."

In the <u>Spring</u>, we plan to visit the <u>Midwest</u>, most specifically <u>South Dakota</u>.

    a. spring
    b. midwest
    c. south dakota
    d. no correction needed

Reading

Directions: Use the following passage to answer questions 1-10.

"So that Nobody Has to Go to School if They Don't Want to"

An Excerpt by Roger Sipher

A decline in standardized test scores is but the most recent indicator that American education is in trouble. One reason for the crisis is that present mandatory-attendance laws force many to attend school that have no wish to be there. Such children have little desire to learn and are so antagonistic to school that neither they nor more highly motivated students receive the quality education that is the birthright of every American. The solution to this problem is simple: Abolish compulsory-attendance laws and allow only those who are committed to getting an education to attend.

Most parents want a high school education for their children. Unfortunately, compulsory attendance hampers the ability of public school officials to enforce legitimate educational and disciplinary policies and thereby make the education a good one. Private schools have no such problem. They can fail or dismiss students, knowing such students can attend public school. Without compulsory attendance, public schools would be freer to oust students whose academic or personal behavior undermines the educational mission of the institution.

Abolition of archaic attendance laws would produce enormous dividends:

- First, it would alert everyone that school is a serious place where one goes to learn. Schools are neither day-care centers nor indoor street corners. Young people who resist learning should stay away; indeed, an end to compulsory schooling would require them to stay away.
- Second, students opposed to learning would not be able to pollute the educational atmosphere for those who want to learn. Teachers could stop policing recalcitrant students and start educating.
- Third, grades would show what they are supposed to: how well a student is learning. Parents could again read report cards and know if their children were making progress.
- Fourth, public esteem for schools would increase. People would stop regarding them as way stations for adolescents and start thinking of them as institutions for educating America's youth.
- Fifth, elementary schools would change because students would find out early they had better learn something or risk flunking out later. Elementary teachers would no longer have to pass their failures on to junior high and high school.
- Sixth, the cost of enforcing compulsory education would be eliminated. Despite enforcement efforts, nearly 15 percent of the school-age children in our largest cities are almost permanently absent from school.

Communities could use these savings to support institutions to deal with young people not in school. If, in the long run, these institutions prove more costly, at least we would not confuse their mission with that of schools. Schools should be for education. At present, they are only tangentially so. They have attempted to serve an all-encompassing social function, trying to be all things to all people. In the process they have failed miserably at what they were originally formed to accomplish.

1. Which of the following statements supports the conclusion that abolishing mandatory attendance laws would prove economical for school districts?

   a. It would eliminate the misconception that schools are day-care centers or indoor street corners.
   b. Public esteem for schools would increase.
   c. The cost of enforcing compulsory education would be eliminated.
   d. Report cards would reflect how well a student is learning.

2. Which of the following statements would the author most likely agree with?

    a. The longer students attend school, the more productive the community will be.

    b. Students should not be forced or entitled to an education.

    c. Truancy officers should be doubled in districts with low attendance rates.

    d. Report cards should reflect the effort of a student, rather than the ability of that student.

3. According to the author, abolishing attendance laws would allow school districts the freedom to _____.

    a. provide counseling to students with poor attendance.

    b. fail or dismiss students who have attendance or discipline issues, which disrupt the education of others.

    c. provide transportation to students unwilling to attend school.

    d. move students from elementary to middle school without proof that learning has occurred.

4. Which of the following is an assumption made by the author?

    a. Private schools can choose to fail or dismiss students.

    b. Nearly 15 percent of the school-age children in our largest cities are almost permanently absent from school.

    c. If we can improve student attendance, we can improve standardized test scores.

    d. Most parents want a high school education for their children.

5. Choose the option that best describes the central idea of the passage.

    a. Standardized test scores would increase if teachers could fail or dismiss students.

    b. Abolishing mandatory attendance laws would create better school environments for the students with a genuine desire to learn.

    c. Report cards should communicate with parents how well a student is learning.

    d. Private schools have an easier time with absenteeism than public schools.

6. Which of the following best summarizes the first paragraph?

    a. American education is in trouble.

    b. Students with little desire to learn are often absent.

    c. Abolishing the mandatory attendance laws would improve the quality of education in schools.

    d. Standardized test scores are the best indicator of student success.

7. Which of the following statements LEAST supports the main idea of the passage?

    a. School is a serious place where one goes to learn.

    b. Students opposed to learning would not be able to pollute the educational atmosphere for those who want to learn.

    c. Grades would show what they are supposed to: how well a student is learning.

    d. Public esteem for schools would increase.

8. According to the text, what effect do mandatory attendance laws have on the esteem of schools?

    a. These laws prove that schools have the right to force education on all minors.

    b. These laws undermine the integrity of schools.

    c. These laws allow students to choose their own path of education.

    d. These laws provide teachers with freedom to grade and dismiss as they see fit.

9. What can we infer from the text?

    a. The author believes that school districts should reexamine their procedures for standardized testing.
    b. The author believes that all students deserve an equal amount of attention from the teacher.
    c. The author believes that stricter attendance laws would improve classroom dynamics.
    d. The author believes that education is a privilege, not a right.

10. Which of the following is a synonym of the word, "recalcitrant," as used in Paragraph 3?

    a. Absent
    b. Organized
    c. Disobedient
    d. Responsible

Directions: Use the following passage to answer questions 11-20.

In 1603, Queen Elizabeth I of England died. She had never married and had no heir, so the throne passed to a distant relative: James Stuart, the son of Elizabeth's cousin and one-time rival for the throne, Mary, Queen of Scots. James was crowned King James I of England. At the time, he was also King James VI of Scotland, and the combination of roles would create a spirit of conflict that haunted the two nations for generations to come.

The conflict developed as a result of rising tensions among the people within the nations, as well as between them. Scholars in the 21st century are far too hasty in dismissing the role of religion in political disputes, but religion undoubtedly played a role in the problems that faced England and Scotland. By the time of James Stuart's succession to the English throne, the English people had firmly embraced the teachings of Protestant theology. Similarly, the Scottish Lowlands were decisively Protestant. In the Scottish Highlands, however, the clans retained their Catholic faith. James acknowledged the Church of England and sanctioned the largely Protestant translation of the Bible that still bears his name.

James's son King Charles I proved himself to be less committed to the Protestant Church of England. Charles married the Catholic Princess Henrietta Maria of France, and there were suspicions among the English and the Lowland Scots that Charles was quietly a Catholic. Charles's own political troubles extended beyond religion in this case, and he was beheaded in 1649. Eventually, his son King Charles II would be crowned, and this Charles is believed to have converted secretly to the Catholic Church. Charles II died without a legitimate heir, and his brother James ascended to the throne as King James II.

James was recognized to be a practicing Catholic, and his commitment to Catholicism would prove to be his downfall. James's wife Mary Beatrice lost a number of children during their infancy, and when she became pregnant again in 1687 the public became concerned. If James had a son, that son would undoubtedly be raised a Catholic, and the English people would not stand for this. Mary gave birth to a son, but the story quickly circulated that the royal child had died, and the child named James's heir was a foundling smuggled in. James, his wife, and his infant son were forced to flee; and James's Protestant daughter Mary was crowned the queen.

In spite of a strong resemblance to the king, the young James was generally rejected among the English and the Lowland Scots, who referred to him as "the Pretender." But in the Highlands the Catholic princeling was welcomed. He inspired a group known as Jacobites, to reflect the Latin version of his name. His own son Charles, known affectionately as Bonnie Prince Charlie, would eventually raise an army and attempt to recapture what he believed to be his throne. The movement was soundly defeated at the Battle of Culloden in 1746, and England and Scotland have remained Protestant ever since.

11. According to the author, the tension between England and Scotland stemmed from what issue?

    a. Politics
    b. Rivalry within the Royal Families
    c. Religion
    d. Boundary disputes

12. According to the text, who was the successor of Queen Elizabeth I?

    a. King Charles I
    b. James Stuart
    c. King James II
    d. Queen Mary

13. Which of the following best summarizes paragraph 4?

    a. The English were determined to convince the son of King James to bring Catholicism to England.
    b. The son of King James died tragically as an infant, leaving no heir to the throne.
    c. James and his wife had only one surviving child, a daughter named Mary.
    d. The English feared that the son of King James would be raised Catholic, causing them to fabricate a story of his death and create a rumor of an illegitimate heir to the throne.

14. Which of the following best compares the religious beliefs of the Scottish Highlands and Lowlands?

    a. Scotland was devoutly Protestant in both the Highlands and Lowlands.
    b. The Highlands were devoutly Protestant, while the Lowlands embraced Catholicism.
    c. The Highlands were accepting of Catholicism, while the Lowlands were devoutly Protestant.
    d. Scotland embraced Catholicism in both the Highlands and the Lowlands.

15. Which of the following choices best describes the relationship between King James I of England and King James VI of Scotland?

    a. They were cousins.
    b. They were brothers.
    c. They were the same person.
    d. King James I was the father of King James VI.

16. Which of the following is a synonym for the term "foundling" as used in paragraph 4?

    a. Orphan
    b. Distant relative
    c. Son
    d. Foreigner

17. What can we infer from the text?

    a. Queen Elizabeth I died at a young age.
    b. King Charles I was not a devout Protestant.
    c. King James II was committed to his family.
    d. King James II was crowned King after his brother, King Charles II, died.

18. According to the text, which statement best supports the author's claim that the downfall of King James II was due to his belief in Catholicism?

    a. He was beheaded for forming the group known as the "Jacobites."
    b. The fear of a Catholic king caused the English to create rumors of an illegitimate son, forcing James to flee England.
    c. He was killed in the Battle of Culloden in 1746.
    d. His wife lost a number of infants, causing a strain in their relationship.

19. Which of the following best describes the term "Jacobites"?

    a. A group of Catholics inspired by the young son of King James II.
    b. A group of Protestants inspired by the young son of King James II.
    c. A group of Protestants inspired by the young Bonnie Prince Charlie.
    d. A group of Catholics inspired by the young son of King Charles II.

20. Choose the option that best describes the central idea of the passage.

    a. King James II tried to fool the English with an illegitimate son as heir to the throne.
    b. The troubles between England and Scotland were largely due to a clash in religious beliefs.
    c. Queen Elizabeth I was the head of a troubled royal family.
    d. James's wife, Mary Beatrice, suffered the loss of many infants.

Directions: Refer to the following passage to answer questions 21–31.

Cultivation of Tomato Plants

Tomato plants should be started in window boxes or greenhouses in late March so that they will be ready for the garden after the last frost. Use a soil of equal parts of sand, peat moss, and manure, and plant the seeds about a quarter of an inch deep. After covering, water them through a cloth to protect the soil and cover the box with a pane of glass. Keep the box in a warm place for a few days, then place it in a sunny window. After the second leaf makes its appearance on the seedling, transplant the plant to another box, placing the seedlings two inches apart. Another alternative is to put the sprouted seedlings in four-inch pots, setting them deeper in the soil than they stood in the seed bed. To make the stem stronger, pinch out the top bud when the seedlings are four or five inches in height.

Finally, place the plants in their permanent positions after they have grown to be twelve or fifteen inches high. When transplanting, parts of some of the longest leaves should be removed. Large plants may be set five or six inches deep.

The soil should be fertilized the previous season. Fresh, stable manure, used as fertilizer, would delay the time of fruiting. To improve the condition of the soil, work in a spade full of old manure to a depth of at least a foot. Nitrate of soda, applied at about two hundred pounds per acre, may be used to give the plant a good start.

Plants grown on supports may be set two feet apart in the row, with the rows three or four feet apart depending upon the variety. Plants not supported by stakes or other methods should be set four feet apart.

Unsupported vines give a lighter yield and much of the fruit is likely to rot during the wet seasons. Use well sharpened stakes about two inches in diameter and five feet long. Drive the stakes into the ground at least six inches from the plants so that the roots will not be injured. Tie the tomato vines to the stakes with strings made out of strips of cloth, as twine is likely to cut them. Care must be taken not to wrap the limbs so tightly as to interfere with their growth. The training should start before the plants begin to trail on the ground.

21. According to the text, why should tomato seedlings be watered through a cloth?

    a. To prevent over-watering
    b. To filter the water
    c. To protect the soil
    d. To warm the water

22. Why does the author suggest pinching out the top bud of the tomato plant when the seedlings are four or five inches in height?

    a. To avoid over-crowding
    b. To allow for more air flow
    c. To avoid rotting
    d. To strengthen the stem

23. Which of the following best describes the text structure of the passage?

    a. Sequence and order
    b. Compare and contrast
    c. Cause and effect
    d. Description

24. Identify the purpose of the author.

    a. To entertain
    b. To inform
    c. To persuade
    d. To compare

25. According to the author, when should tomato plants be moved to their permanent positions?

    a. After the second leaf makes its appearance.
    b. After the first fertilization.
    c. When the seedling starts to sprout.
    d. After they have grown to be 12 to 15 inches high.

26. Which of the following choices best defines "yield" as used in the last paragraph?

    a. A color or hue
    b. The amount produced
    c. The height of a plant
    d. An explosive force

27. Identify a synonym for the term "fruiting" as used in Paragraph 3.
   a. Ripening
   b. Decaying
   c. Watering
   d. Decomposing

28. Why does the author dissuade the use of twine?
   a. Because it gets too hot in the sun
   b. Because it may cut the tomato vines
   c. Because it may wrap the tomato vines too tightly
   d. Because it is not porous

29. All of the following are part of the recommended soil EXCEPT _____.
   a. clay.
   b. peat moss.
   c. manure.
   d. sand.

30. Choose the option that best describes the author's pattern of organization for Paragraphs 1 and 2.
   a. Cause and effect
   b. Problem and solution
   c. Sequential
   d. Persuasive

31. The author would most likely agree with which of the following statements?
   a. Unsupported plants should be set farther apart than supported plants.
   b. Freshly fertilized soil should be used when planting tomatoes.
   c. Twine should be used to tie tomato vines to stakes.
   d. Tomato harvesting should begin in May.

Directions: Refer to the following passage to answer questions 32–41.

Stories have been a part of the world since the beginning of recorded time. For centuries before the invention of the printing press, stories of the world were passed down throughout the generations through oral tradition. With the invention of the printing press, which made written material available to a wide range of audiences, books were mass-produced and introduced into greater society. Before the printing press was invented, books had to be hand copied, which made books very difficult to make and very costly as a result.

For the last several centuries, books have been at the forefront of education and entertainment. With the invention of the Internet, reliance on books for information quickly changed. Soon, almost everything that anyone needed to know could be accessed through the Internet. Large printed volumes of encyclopedias became unnecessary, as all of the information was easily available on the Internet.

Despite the progression of the Internet, printed media was still very popular in the forms of both fiction and non-fiction books. Similarly, newspapers are a format of reading material that has been widespread in availability and use. While waiting for an appointment, enduring a several-hour flight, or relaxing before sleep, books, magazines, and newspapers have been a reliable and convenient source of entertainment, and one that society has not been willing to give up.

With the progression and extreme convenience of technology, printed books are soon going to become a thing of the past. Inventions such as the iPad from Apple and the Kindle have made the need for any kind of printed media unnecessary. With a rechargeable battery, a large screen, and the ability to have several books saved on file, electronic options will soon take over and society will no longer see printed books.

Some people still cling to the old format of printed books as they enjoy owning and reading from paper materials. Although some people may say that the act of reading is not complete without turning a page, sliding a finger across the screen or pressing a button to read more onto the next page is just as satisfying to the reader. The iPad and Kindle are devices that have qualities similar to a computer and can be used for so much more than just reading. These devices are therefore better than books because they have multiple uses.

In a cultural society that is part of the world and due to a longstanding tradition, stories will always be an important way to communicate ideas and provide information and entertainment. Centuries ago, stories could only be remembered and retold through speech. Printed media changed the way the world communicated and was connected, and now, as we move forward with technology, it is only a matter of time before we must say goodbye to the printed past and welcome the digital and electronic future.

32. Before the invention of the printing press, books were costly to make because _____.
   a. Paper was scarce.
   b. Books had to be handwritten.
   c. People preferred spoken storytelling.
   d. Books were difficult to ship.

33. How are the following two sentences related?

Sentence 1: While waiting for an appointment, enduring a several-hour flight, or relaxing before sleep, books, magazines, and newspapers have been a reliable and convenient source of entertainment, and one that society has not been willing to give up.

Sentence 2: With a rechargeable battery, a large screen, and the ability to have several books saved on file, electronic options will soon take over and society will no longer see printed books.

   a. Sentence 2 clarifies sentence 1.
   b. Sentence 1 supports the main idea of sentence 2.
   c. They are contradictory of one another.
   d. Sentence 2 offers a solution to a problem presented in sentence 1.

34. According to the text, why are printed encyclopedias no longer necessary?
   a. Because the information is outdated
   b. Because all of the information can be found on the Internet
   c. Because libraries could no longer store them
   d. Because they are too expensive to print

35. Why does the author feel that electronic devices are better than books?

a. Because they have multiple uses
b. Because they store more than one book at a time
c. Because they are easier to transport
d. Because they are rechargeable

36. What act is the author describing in the phrase, "sliding a finger across the screen" in Paragraph 5?

a. Cleaning and maintaining an electronic device
b. Charging an electronic device
c. Turning the page of an electronic book
d. Turning the page of a newspaper

37. From the text we can infer that the author _____.

a. believes books are more enjoyable than electronic devices.
b. would rather read a newspaper than a Kindle.
c. prefers informational text over fiction.
d. is ready to move forward with technological advances.

38. According to the text, stories provide all of the following, EXCEPT _____.

a. communicating ideas.
b. providing information.
c. support the need for electronic devices.
d. entertainment.

39. Which of the following best defines "enduring," as used in Paragraph 3?

a. Reading
b. Traveling
c. Tolerating
d. Vacationing

40. The sentence "With the invention of the printing press, which made written material available to wide ranges of audiences, books were mass-produced and introduced into greater society," is used to show _____.

a. sequence.
b. cause and effect.
c. problem and solution.
d. compare and contrast.

41. According to the text, the first stories were told…

a. through handwritten books.
b. through printed material.
c. through electronic devices.
d. through speech.

Directions: Refer to the following passage to answer questions 42–50.

The process of making wine is one that is as old as history itself. For some wineries, the process has been the same for hundreds of years and is a highly valued and heavily guarded secret. Every winemaker has his or her own materials, ingredients, and processes that lend to the creation of a unique product. Modern research has taken place to look at the connection between the science behind winemaking and the resulting artwork.

Some wine aficionados prize the flavor of oak, usually imparted to the beverage through aging in wooden barrels. An alternative process, aging in metal casks with macerated wood chips, provides a stronger wood flavor in less time and therefore is less expensive. To test consumer preferences for wines processed in this manner, a survey of 618 people living in several East Coast cities was conducted early last year. Participants took a blind taste test of three samples of Oregon Pinot Noir. One sample was aged using macerated wood chips, one sample was aged under oak, and a third sample, the control, was aged in a metal tank. A questionnaire asked subjects to rate the wines and then asked a variety of other questions aimed at categorizing their consumption habits.

Although a variety of factors influenced wine preference, the test exposed a pattern concerning a preference for strongly wood-flavored wines. A large proportion of those persons interviewed (45%) did not care for the tannic wines. However, a sizable minority of 25% liked them very much, and preferred the tannic wines to the other samples. Younger consumers particularly fell into this category. Connoisseurs reported greater appreciation for wines aged "under oak," or in normal oak barrels.

Many high-quality wines are aged under oak today. Nonetheless, this process is time consuming; as a result, it makes wines more expensive. This survey demonstrated that price is very important in the buying decision, especially for people without extensive knowledge regarding wine. Many consumers are more concerned with price differences than with subtle differences in flavor. This trend defines a market segment that might be well served by wines aged with wood chips.

Although wine making has been a generally unchanging tradition, modern research and practices may be able to change the standard methods of wine making. In turn, these new methods make the process more efficient and will help to make unique and high-quality wine available for everyone at a much lower cost.

42. Which of the following wine-making processes produce the strongest flavor of oak in the least amount of time?
    a. Storing the wine in oak barrels
    b. Storing the wine with wood chips
    c. Storing the wine in metal containers
    d. Adding chemicals to the wine as it is mixed

43. Modern research will affect the wine industry in each of the following ways EXCEPT _____.
    a. the process of making wine will be more efficient.
    b. the cost of purchasing wine will decrease.
    c. the shipping of wine will improve.
    d. the quality of wine will improve.

44. According to the survey, consumers are most interested in what aspect of purchasing wine?

    a. Price
    b. Taste
    c. Process
    d. Vintage year

45. According to the text, wine that is aged under oak is expensive because _____.

    a. it is time-consuming.
    b. wood barrels are expensive.
    c. wood chips are in high demand.
    d. tannic wine is becoming increasingly popular.

46. Choose the option that best defines the term "aficionados," as used in Paragraph 2.

    a. A person who participates in a taste-testing survey
    b. A type of wine
    c. A person who is very knowledgeable or enthusiastic about a topic
    d. A process for creating wine

47. Which of the following best describes the purpose of the text?

    a. To entertain
    b. To inform
    c. To persuade
    d. To solve a problem

48. All of the following samples were part of the taste test EXCEPT _____.

    a. a sample that was aged under oak.
    b. a sample with macerated wood chips.
    c. a sample that contained pomegranate.
    d. a sample that was aged in a metal tank.

49. According to the survey, which group of people preferred the tannic wines?

    a. The younger population
    b. The wine aficionados
    c. The older population
    d. The East Coast population

50. Based on the sentence, "A questionnaire asked subjects to rate the wines and then asked a variety of other questions aimed at categorizing their consumption habits," we can infer…

    a. the surveyors were only interested in the favorite-tasting wine.
    b. the surveyors were interested in analyzing how people with various consumption habits preferred their wine.
    c. surveyors were interested in the amount of time it took taste-testers to complete the survey.
    d. surveyors were interested in the education level of taste-testers.

Essay Questions

1. In peaceful protest of what they believe to be oppression in America, many athletes of the National Football League have decided to kneel rather than standing for our National Anthem. Some viewers see this as a platform for public figures to bring awareness and change, while others view it as a disrespectful action towards our country, our flag, and those who serve and protect. Do athletes have the right to protest during the National Anthem? Does it disrespect our country, flag, and military?

2. The American Academy of Pediatrics recently announced that children as young as 18 months old can benefit from high-value, academic screen time, when supervised by an adult. Others argue that introducing electronics to children at such a young age will limit their ability to interact in the real world as they grow and mature. Do the advantages of educational programs outweigh the disadvantages?

Answer Key and Explanations

Writing

1. B: A modifier is a word that can describe or change the meaning of another word or phrase in a sentence. A modifier should be placed next to the word or phrase it is describing. In choice B, the modifier (hot) is placed next to the mug it is describing, making B our correct answer.

2. A: When a modifier is misplaced, it gives an attribute to an unintended word or phrase. The sentence, "I found a gold ring walking home" uses the modifier "walking" to describe the ring. Instead, we should write the sentence as, "Walking home, I found a gold ring."

3. B: Parallel structure uses the same pattern of words when describing related events. Here, the words used to describe Chase's actions are "watered" and "mowed." The only choice that fits this pattern is choice B, "vacuumed," because it is written in past tense and does not have a pronoun preceding it.

4. C: Parallelism uses the same tense of words to create a pattern in writing structure. Here, three of the answer choices end in "–ing," insinuating present tense. Choice C, "ran" is written in past tense and therefore does not establish parallelism with the other choices.

5. A: Parallelism requires that verbs be written in the same form or tense. Choice A does not meet this criterion because Jose wants to return the item (which shows a desire for the future), yet states that he already spoke to a manager (insinuating past tense).

6. C: A complete sentence must contain a subject and a verb. A fragment may look like a sentence, but it is missing one of these components. Choice C contains the fragment, "The large horse with a beautiful mane," which is missing the verb.

7. A: A comma splice occurs when only a comma connects two independent clauses. Choice C can eliminate the comma splice by separating the thoughts into two complete sentences, by using a semicolon to separate the thoughts, or by rewriting the sentence as "Many athletes have personal trainers, because trainers help them stay fit in the off-season."

8. C: A run-on sentence contains two complete thoughts without appropriate punctuation separating them. Choice C contains two complete thoughts without any separation. We can rewrite it as, "I learned what marine biologists do, and I think I would like to pursue that career."

9. D: A syntax error is an error in the usage of language. Here, the phrase "intensive purposes" is mistaken for "intents and purposes."

10. B: The question, "Do pigs fly?" has an obvious answer, which does not require a response. It is often used to make a point that the answer to some other question is undoubtedly "no." This type of language is known as rhetorical.

11. B: The error is a misplaced modifier. Did the professor make this statement *on* Monday, or will the papers be *returned* on Monday? The sentence should be rewritten as, "On Monday, the professor said she would return our papers." Or, "The professor said she would return our papers on Monday."

12. D: The sentence explains that James packed an umbrella to solve the problem of getting wet in the rain. This type of organizational structure is known as problem and solution.

13. A: A sentence must contain a subject and a predicate (or verb). "A giant Rhodesian Ridgeback" is a fragment because it is missing a verb.

14. B: We can use context clues to determine that the hikers quickly fed the dog to satisfy his or her hunger. We can then conclude that "emaciated" must refer to the dog's physical condition, known by his or her thin appearance.

15. D: The conjunction, "but" is used to show a contrast in something that has already been stated. Here, we know that Stacey's feelings about eating differ from her feelings about cooking. If she enjoys eating, then she must detest cooking.

16. C: Fiona's smirk insinuates that she was pleased with the election results. This leads us to determine that the word "content," as used in this sentence, most closely illustrates Fiona's satisfaction.

17. B: Our answer has to be "through" as it is the only choice that provides the correct spelling and meaning for running past the defense.

18. B: "Than" is used to show a comparison, while "then" is used to show sequence or a moment in time and "thin" refers to a slim size. Here, we're comparing the number of baskets each player made, so "than" is the correct choice.

19. C: "They're" is a contraction used in place of "they are." Because reading the sentence as "They are going to wash the dishes after they clear the table" makes sense, we can choose C as our answer.

20. D: The ability to read from a long distance refers to good sight. "Site" refers to a location and "cite" means to refer to something, so "vision" is the only correct choice.

21. B: When we "infer," we make a conclusion based on evidence or reasoning, rather than explicitly stated information. In this sentence, the jury inferred guilt based on the actions of the accused.

22. C: The sentence is showing how flood insurance gives the homeowner comfort in knowing that his or her valuables are protected. Another way of saying this would be "peace of mind," but not "piece of mind," which refers to a portion of one's mind.

23. B: Jargon refers to words or phrases that are linked to a specific trade. We can reasonably assume that electricians would speak to fellow electricians in a way that is specific to their expertise.

24. B: A writer's tone is used to convey the attitude of an author or character. For example, the phrase "nice haircut" can be used to convey a sincere comment or a sarcastic insult, depending on the author's tone.

25. A: The author describes the character as fidgeting with trembling knees and a quivering voice. All of these descriptors depict a tone of anxiety or unease.

26. A: The word "often" is typically used in the present tense. Once we know we're looking for a word in the present tense, we can conclude that "jogs" is our best choice based on the sentence structure already in place. None of the remaining choices is grammatically correct.

27. D: When we insert each of the answer choices in the blank space, "has been" is the only choice that preserves the tense and sentence structure of the text.

28. B: We should never shift verb tense in a sentence unless we are showing a change in time. This sentence is simply informing the reader about leopard geckos and does not require a shift in verb tense.

29. D: The sentence has a change of time, offering information from 2010 and relating it to today. The time change necessitates a shift in verb tense, therefore no change is needed.

30. C: The first sentence used the verb "protested," which is past tense. Because the sentence does not show a change in time, there is no need to shift the verb tense. We need to change "gather" to "gathered."

31. A: In this sentence, the three wolves form a plural subject, so we must choose a plural form of the verb.

32. D: The word "to" signals the use of the infinitive form of the verb ("to attend").

33. D: The pronouns "whose" and "his" both refer to the antecedent, Mayor Williams. Both pronouns are used correctly, so there is no correction needed.

34. B: Here, the pronoun is referring to the rainbow, which is a singular noun (neither masculine or feminine), so we must use the pronoun "its." To clarify, "it's" refers to the contraction of "it is," which does not make sense here.

35. C: The error in this sentence is known as a pronoun shift, which occurs when a sentence starts with one pronoun, then shifts to another. Here, the sentence starts with the pronoun "you," then shifts to "most." We can fix this by replacing "most" with the already established pronoun, "you."

36. C: The sentence contains a pronoun shift, which needs to be addressed. The start of the sentence introduces the pronoun "we." However, toward the end of the sentence, it shifts to "you." This error can be corrected by maintaining the use of "we" as the designated pronoun.

37. D: The sentence contains two different antecedents, each of which the pronoun "she" might represent. The ambiguous pronoun reference makes the sentence unclear, which leaves the reader to wonder which girl the principal is suspicious of.

38. B: When selecting the pronoun for an unnamed animal, "that" is the preferred choice. However, if the animal is named, the pronoun should be adjusted to "who."

39. A: The pronoun "they" is used in place of the subject, therefore it is known as a subjective pronoun.

40. C: Here, the pronoun "her" is showing ownership of the shoe, so is it a possessive pronoun.

41. C: "Quick" is an adjective used to describe a noun, while "quickly" is an adverb used to describe a verb. Because the sentence is describing the verb "ran," we need to use the adverb "quickly."

42. B: The word "lively" is used to describe the concert, which is a noun. A word used to describe a noun is an adjective. Although words ending in "-ly" are often adverbs, they can on occasion be adjectives instead.

- 110 -

43. C: The sentence is comparing the first apple of the season to all of the other apples. Because we are describing the apple against a group of other apples, as opposed to just one, we need the superlative form of juicy, which is "juiciest."

44. B: When comparing only two objects, we must use a comparative descriptor. In this sentence, we are comparing an elephant to a mouse, so "heavier" must be used to complete the sentence.

45. A: The word "definitely" is misspelled in this sentence as "definately."

46. D: The sentence contains no errors, so no correction is needed.

47. B: Semicolons are used to separate two independent clauses in an effort to avoid run-on sentences. Here, the second clause depends on the first clause, making the semicolon incorrect.

48. D: In this sentence, "child's" is being used to show possession of the skin, necessitating the need for an apostrophe.

49. C: The first part of a dinosaur name, known as the genus, must always be capitalized. We can correct this sentence by capitalizing "Titanosaur."

50. A: Seasons are never capitalized, so we can correct this sentence by *not* capitalizing "spring."

Reading

1. C: Although all four options are arguably benefits to eliminating mandatory attendance laws, the term "economical" tells us we're looking for a cost-effective advantage. According to the author, the cost of enforcing compulsory education is money ill-spent and could be better spent on students who *want* to be there.

2. B: According to the author, many problems that arise in schools are a direct result of students who are forced to be there. The author believes that attendance laws should be abolished in order to make education more valuable to students with a desire to learn.

3. B: The author believes that education is failing because teachers and schools spend far too much time disciplining behavior issues and mandating attendance. Teachers could better serve conscientious students if given the opportunity to fail or dismiss those who are disrupting the education of others.

4. D: An assumption is something we believe to be true because it is something we have been taught to believe and do not question. Here, the author is assuming that most parents want a high school education for their children. There is no evidence in the text supporting that claim, but the author believes it to be true based on his own experiences and beliefs.

5. B: Although all four options reflect the author's beliefs, only one of them describes the central idea, or main idea, of the writing. The author is trying to prove that abolishing mandatory attendance laws would create better school environments for the students with a genuine desire to learn. The other answer choices are used as supporting evidence to reinforce that claim.

6. C: A summary is a brief statement used to describe the main idea of writing, or a portion of that writing. The first paragraph of this article mentions all four choices, but the main idea is that abolishing mandatory attendance laws would improve the quality of education in schools. The other answer choices list ways in which the abolition of these laws could improve the climate of education or reasons why this abolition is necessary.

7. C: The author's main idea is that abolishing mandatory attendance laws would allow teachers the ability to dismiss disruptive students, preserving the sanctity of schools as a place for students to receive an esteemed education. Bullet three does not support that specific claim, but instead describes an issue with the grading of such students.

8. B: According to the text, mandatory attendance laws undermine the integrity of schools because teachers have no choice but to provide all students, regardless of behavior or attendance, the same educational opportunities. When there is no recourse for disrupting the learning environment, schools can be perceived as day cares or, as the author described, "indoor street corners."

9. D: An inference is defined as a conclusion reached on the basis of evidence and reasoning. Throughout the passage the author has provided several reasons why students with behavior and/or attendance concerns should not be afforded the opportunity to disrupt the education of others. From these claims we can infer that the author believes education is a privilege to those who want to put in the effort and not a birthright of every juvenile in a community.

10. C: Context clues are hints we can use within an author's writing to determine the meaning of an unknown word. The author writes, "Teachers could stop policing recalcitrant students and start educating." We can use context clues to determine that the term "recalcitrant" most similarly describes students who are disobedient, if they require the policing of teachers.

11. C: According to the author, the major clash between England and Scotland stemmed from religious differences. The countries clashed over Catholic and Protestant beliefs, causing tension among the citizens as well as members of the royal families.

12. B: According to the text, Queen Elizabeth I died in 1603. With no heir to her throne, the son of her cousin, James Stuart, was crowned King.

13. D: Paragraph 4 states that James and his wife lost many children during infancy. His son survived infancy, but the English feared that he would be raised Catholic and eventually become king, influencing Catholicism throughout England. To avoid this, they fabricated a story of his death and created a rumor that the king had replaced the young prince with an imposter, forcing James, his wife, and their young son to flee.

14. C: While England and the Scottish Lowlands were Protestant, the Highlands were accepting of Catholicism and even formed a group of Catholic followers known as "Jacobites."

15. C: When Queen Elizabeth I of England died, she had no heir. Therefore, her cousin's son, James, became King of England. He was named King James I of England, while already crowned King James VI of Scotland.

16. A: In paragraph 4, the author writes, "Mary gave birth to a son, but the story quickly circulated that the royal child had died, and the child named James's heir was a foundling smuggled in." We can use context clues to determine that the rumored child was illegitimate, and therefore most likely an orphan with no lawful rights to the throne.

17. C: An inference is a conclusion we make based on evidence and reasoning without the text explicitly giving us the information. The text states that King James II was being accused of having an illegitimate son as heir to the throne. The text also states that, rather than risk the safety of his family, James chose to flee with his wife and son, relinquishing his rightful seat as the King of England. From this, we can infer that King James II was committed to his family.

18. B: King James II was believed to be raising his son as a Catholic. The English were so fearful at the thought of a Catholic king that they created rumors of an illegitimate son, forcing James to flee England and abdicate his throne.

19. A: The term "Jacobites" refers to a group of Catholics inspired by the young son of King James II. The group was named to reflect the Latin version of James' name and gathered to practice Catholicism in the Highlands.

20. B: Although it is true that true that Mary Beatrice suffered the loss of many infants and Queen Elizabeth I was part of a troubled royal family, neither of these statements summarize the central idea of the passage. The author's main assertion is that the troubles between England and Scotland were largely due to a clash in religious beliefs.

21. C: According to the text, watering tomato plants through a cloth helps to protect the soil.

22. D: The author states, "to make the stem stronger, pinch out the top bud when the seedlings are four or five inches in height." Therefore, the purpose of pinching out the top bud is to strengthen the stem.

23. A: A nonfiction passage that is written to reflect the sequence and order text structure gives readers a chronological list of events or a list of steps in a procedure. Here, the text is describing the process for growing tomatoes as a step-by-step procedure, making it a sequence and order text structure.

24. B: The author is trying to convey the best way to grow tomatoes. The article is not persuasive, nor is it attempting to entertain the reader. The purpose of the text is strictly to inform the reader.

25. D: According to the text, tomato plants should be moved to their permanent position after they have grown to be 12 to 15 inches high. The author recommends removing parts of the larger leaves at this time as well.

26. B: The term "yield" refers to the amount of tomatoes produced by unsupported vines. Here, the text is stating that unsupported vines will produce fewer tomatoes than supported vines.

27. A: The author is giving advice in an effort to "avoid a delay in fruiting." Using context clues, we can determine that fruiting is something that we *want* to occur in a timely manner. The only answer choice that describes a desired part of the harvesting process is "ripening," therefore we can conclude that ripening is a synonym for fruiting.

28. B: The author warns that wrapping tomato vines in twine may cut them. Instead, the author suggests using strips of cloth to tie the vines.

29. A: According to the text, tomato plants should be harvested using a soil made of equal parts sand, peat moss, and manure. Clay is not listed as a recommended part of the harvesting process.

30. C: The information is organized in a way that describes the step-by-step process for harvesting tomatoes. This type of text is described as sequential writing.

31. A: In Paragraph 4, the author states "Plants grown on supports may be set two feet apart in the row, with the rows three or four feet apart depending upon the variety. Plants not supported by stakes or other methods should be set four feet apart." We can summarize this information to conclude that unsupported vines should be set farther apart than supported vines.

32. B: Before the invention of the printing press, books had to be handwritten, making them difficult to create and costly to produce.

33. C: Sentence 1 states that printed materials are still valued and cherished in our society. Sentence 2 asserts that printed materials are a thing of the past. The points contradict one another, making the sentences contradictory.

34. B: Volumes of encyclopedias are large and cumbersome. They are no longer necessary to store and refer to because all of the information in them can easily be found on the Internet. To clarify further, although the information on the Internet is more current, encyclopedias being outdated is not a reason stated in the text, so choice A cannot be our answer here.

35. A: The author states that electronic devices can store more than one book at a time, as well as serve many other purposes. Because these devices have multiple uses, the author believes they are better than books.

36. C: In order to read the next page of an electronic book, most devices require the reader to swipe his or her finger across the screen. The term "sliding a finger across the screen" refers to turning the page of an electronic book.

37. D: The author concludes his passage with the sentence, "Printed media changed the way the world communicated and was connected, and now, as we move forward with technology, it is only a matter of time before we must say goodbye to the printed past and welcome the digital and electronic future." From this, we can infer that the author is ready to move forward with advances in the world of technology.

38. C: Since the beginning of time, stories have been a way for people to share ideas, information, and entertain one another. It wasn't until recent technology that devices have proved their worth in the world of storytelling.

39. C: The phrase "enduring a long flight" refers to tolerating a lengthy plane ride. Here, the referral of an unpleasant travel experience is used to provide an example of when people enjoy printed material to pass the time.

40. B: The sentence cites the invention of the printing press as the reason for books being produced at a faster rate, thus giving them the opportunity to be dispersed to larger audiences. This shows cause and effect, where the cause is the invention of the printing press, and the effect is the widespread distribution of books.

41. D: According to the text, the first stories were told from generation to generation through speech. Stories needed to be remembered and retold in order to keep their legacy alive. The invention of the printing press changed all of that.

42. B: According to the text, storing wine in metal casks with macerated wood chips provides a stronger wood flavor in less time and therefore is less expensive.

43. C: The author states, "these new methods make the process more efficient and will help to make unique and high-quality wine available for everyone at a much lower cost." The article does not discuss how the shipping of wine will be affected.

44. A: Results from the survey concluded, "Many consumers are more concerned with price differences than with subtle differences in flavor."

45. A: Wine that is aged under oak tends to cost more money because the process is time-consuming.

46. C: A wine aficionado refers to a person who is very knowledgeable and interested in the production and consumption of wine.

47. B: The article is written to inform the reader of different processes for making wine, as well as to describe the preferences of wine drinkers by providing feedback from a blind taste test. The text does not try to persuade the reader to feel a certain way, nor is it written to entertain.

48. C: The text states that one of the wines involved in the taste test included macerated wood chips, one sample was aged under oak, and a third sample was aged in a metal tank. There is no mention of pomegranate being a part of the taste test.

49. A: According to the text, 25% of those surveyed preferred tannic wines. The younger population represented the majority of that 25%.

50. B: The text states, "A questionnaire asked subjects to rate the wines and then asked a variety of other questions aimed at categorizing their consumption habits." Because surveyors took the time to collect information about consumption habits, we can infer that they were interested in analyzing how people with various consumption habits preferred the tastes of different wines.

Essay Sample Response #1

Many athletes of the National Football League have decided to kneel rather than standing for our national anthem. Most of these athletes are kneeling during the anthem in an effort to peacefully protest the unfair treatment and oppression of certain groups within our borders. While I agree with the need for change in America, I believe that kneeling during the national anthem is a disrespectful action toward our country, our flag, and those who serve and protect.

Historically, the national anthem is played as a sign of respect and gratitude for our Armed Forces. It is a way for America to stand at attention and show their appreciation for the men and women who have fought and continue to fight for our country. The anthem also shows the greatest respect toward those who have lost their lives protecting our freedoms. Kneeling during this time minimizes the sacrifices that these brave soldiers have made and continue to make for the citizens of the United States of America.

The athletes protesting the anthem have a right to show their discontent with oppression in America; however, they should do so using a different platform and in a way that does not disrespect those who have selflessly fought to protect our freedoms. Perhaps these athletes can volunteer their time in educating people on the unfair treatment of certain subgroups, or donate money to fund programs that are already making great strides towards equality in America. There are many avenues athletes can take in an effort to shine a light on these issues, but it seems that kneeling is their only action.

In conclusion, I support the athletes' right to bring awareness to causes that they feel strongly about and urge them to use their fame to improve cohesiveness and unite the citizens of our great country. However, during the national anthem is not the time or place to make a political statement. Kneeling does not solve the problem; it only adds more of a divide in a country that is already fractured.

Essay Sample Response #2

The American Academy of Pediatrics recently announced that children as young as 18 months old can benefit from high-value, academic screen time, when supervised by an adult. Though screen time may prove advantageous for curious minds, it also has the power to negatively affect the social development of very young children. In an ever-evolving world, parents often find themselves caught between wanting their children to succeed in a technology-rich environment without losing the ability to interact face-to-face. When used responsibly, the advantages of screen time definitely outweigh the disadvantages.

The biggest factor of the screen time debate lies in what people consider to be "screen time." Many critics depict screen time as non-educational videos or mindless games. These critics suggest the image of a child placed on a chair and given a tablet, for the sole purpose of keeping that child entertained and/or quiet for long periods of time. If this were the case, then screen time would absolutely be disadvantageous for developing minds. This depiction, however, is certainly not the type of activity that The American Academy of Pediatrics is endorsing.

For many parents, screen time consists of educational programs, most of which are interactive and involve young learners in a host of activities. In addition to videos, there are countless applications that are geared towards young learners that actually teach and practice concepts such as shape recognition, counting, phonics, and even reading. When used with parental supervision, these videos and applications can aid parents in creating educational environments at home, even if the parent has no experience "teaching" these skills.

Each year, the world depends on technology more and more. Young children should absolutely be exposed to this technology at a young age so that they are comfortable using the devices that they will eventually rely on for everyday tasks. In addition, educational screen time can provide parents and caretakers with endless opportunities to teach and engage in ways that might not be possible without the assistance of technology. When used appropriately, the advantages of electronic devices most certainly outweigh the disadvantages.

How to Overcome Test Anxiety

Just the thought of taking a test is enough to make most people a little nervous. A test is an important event that can have a long-term impact on your future, so it's important to take it seriously and it's natural to feel anxious about performing well. But just because anxiety is normal, that doesn't mean that it's helpful in test taking, or that you should simply accept it as part of your life. Anxiety can have a variety of effects. These effects can be mild, like making you feel slightly nervous, or severe, like blocking your ability to focus or remember even a simple detail.

If you experience test anxiety—whether severe or mild—it's important to know how to beat it. To discover this, first you need to understand what causes test anxiety.

Causes of Test Anxiety

While we often think of anxiety as an uncontrollable emotional state, it can actually be caused by simple, practical things. One of the most common causes of test anxiety is that a person does not feel adequately prepared for their test. This feeling can be the result of many different issues such as poor study habits or lack of organization, but the most common culprit is time management. Starting to study too late, failing to organize your study time to cover all of the material, or being distracted while you study will mean that you're not well prepared for the test. This may lead to cramming the night before, which will cause you to be physically and mentally exhausted for the test. Poor time management also contributes to feelings of stress, fear, and hopelessness as you realize you are not well prepared but don't know what to do about it.

Other times, test anxiety is not related to your preparation for the test but comes from unresolved fear. This may be a past failure on a test, or poor performance on tests in general. It may come from comparing yourself to others who seem to be performing better or from the stress of living up to expectations. Anxiety may be driven by fears of the future—how failure on this test would affect your educational and career goals. These fears are often completely irrational, but they can still negatively impact your test performance.

> **Review Video:** 3 Reasons You Have Test Anxiety
> Visit mometrix.com/academy and enter code: 428468

Elements of Test Anxiety

As mentioned earlier, test anxiety is considered to be an emotional state, but it has physical and mental components as well. Sometimes you may not even realize that you are suffering from test anxiety until you notice the physical symptoms. These can include trembling hands, rapid heartbeat, sweating, nausea, and tense muscles. Extreme anxiety may lead to fainting or vomiting. Obviously, any of these symptoms can have a negative impact on testing. It is important to recognize them as soon as they begin to occur so that you can address the problem before it damages your performance.

> **Review Video: 3 Ways to Tell You Have Test Anxiety**
> Visit mometrix.com/academy and enter code: 927847

The mental components of test anxiety include trouble focusing and inability to remember learned information. During a test, your mind is on high alert, which can help you recall information and stay focused for an extended period of time. However, anxiety interferes with your mind's natural processes, causing you to blank out, even on the questions you know well. The strain of testing during anxiety makes it difficult to stay focused, especially on a test that may take several hours. Extreme anxiety can take a huge mental toll, making it difficult not only to recall test information but even to understand the test questions or pull your thoughts together.

> **Review Video: How Test Anxiety Affects Memory**
> Visit mometrix.com/academy and enter code: 609003

Effects of Test Anxiety

Test anxiety is like a disease—if left untreated, it will get progressively worse. Anxiety leads to poor performance, and this reinforces the feelings of fear and failure, which in turn lead to poor performances on subsequent tests. It can grow from a mild nervousness to a crippling condition. If allowed to progress, test anxiety can have a big impact on your schooling, and consequently on your future.

Test anxiety can spread to other parts of your life. Anxiety on tests can become anxiety in any stressful situation, and blanking on a test can turn into panicking in a job situation. But fortunately, you don't have to let anxiety rule your testing and determine your grades. There are a number of relatively simple steps you can take to move past anxiety and function normally on a test and in the rest of life.

> **Review Video: How Test Anxiety Impacts Your Grades**
> Visit mometrix.com/academy and enter code: 939819

Physical Steps for Beating Test Anxiety

While test anxiety is a serious problem, the good news is that it can be overcome. It doesn't have to control your ability to think and remember information. While it may take time, you can begin taking steps today to beat anxiety.

Just as your first hint that you may be struggling with anxiety comes from the physical symptoms, the first step to treating it is also physical. Rest is crucial for having a clear, strong mind. If you are tired, it is much easier to give in to anxiety. But if you establish good sleep habits, your body and mind will be ready to perform optimally, without the strain of exhaustion. Additionally, sleeping well helps you to retain information better, so you're more likely to recall the answers when you see the test questions.

Getting good sleep means more than going to bed on time. It's important to allow your brain time to relax. Take study breaks from time to time so it doesn't get overworked, and don't study right before bed. Take time to rest your mind before trying to rest your body, or you may find it difficult to fall asleep.

> **Review Video: The Importance of Sleep for Your Brain**
> Visit mometrix.com/academy and enter code: 319338

Along with sleep, other aspects of physical health are important in preparing for a test. Good nutrition is vital for good brain function. Sugary foods and drinks may give a burst of energy but this burst is followed by a crash, both physically and emotionally. Instead, fuel your body with protein and vitamin-rich foods.

Also, drink plenty of water. Dehydration can lead to headaches and exhaustion, especially if your brain is already under stress from the rigors of the test. Particularly if your test is a long one, drink water during the breaks. And if possible, take an energy-boosting snack to eat between sections.

> **Review Video: How Diet Can Affect your Mood**
> Visit mometrix.com/academy and enter code: 624317

Along with sleep and diet, a third important part of physical health is exercise. Maintaining a steady workout schedule is helpful, but even taking 5-minute study breaks to walk can help get your blood pumping faster and clear your head. Exercise also releases endorphins, which contribute to a positive feeling and can help combat test anxiety.

When you nurture your physical health, you are also contributing to your mental health. If your body is healthy, your mind is much more likely to be healthy as well. So take time to rest, nourish your body with healthy food and water, and get moving as much as possible. Taking these physical steps will make you stronger and more able to take the mental steps necessary to overcome test anxiety.

> **Review Video: How to Stay Healthy and Prevent Test Anxiety**
> Visit mometrix.com/academy and enter code: 877894

Mental Steps for Beating Test Anxiety

Working on the mental side of test anxiety can be more challenging, but as with the physical side, there are clear steps you can take to overcome it. As mentioned earlier, test anxiety often stems from lack of preparation, so the obvious solution is to prepare for the test. Effective studying may be the most important weapon you have for beating test anxiety, but you can and should employ several other mental tools to combat fear.

First, boost your confidence by reminding yourself of past success—tests or projects that you aced. If you're putting as much effort into preparing for this test as you did for those, there's no reason you should expect to fail here. Work hard to prepare; then trust your preparation.

Second, surround yourself with encouraging people. It can be helpful to find a study group, but be sure that the people you're around will encourage a positive attitude. If you spend time with others who are anxious or cynical, this will only contribute to your own anxiety. Look for others who are motivated to study hard from a desire to succeed, not from a fear of failure.

Third, reward yourself. A test is physically and mentally tiring, even without anxiety, and it can be helpful to have something to look forward to. Plan an activity following the test, regardless of the outcome, such as going to a movie or getting ice cream.

When you are taking the test, if you find yourself beginning to feel anxious, remind yourself that you know the material. Visualize successfully completing the test. Then take a few deep, relaxing breaths and return to it. Work through the questions carefully but with confidence, knowing that you are capable of succeeding.

Developing a healthy mental approach to test taking will also aid in other areas of life. Test anxiety affects more than just the actual test—it can be damaging to your mental health and even contribute to depression. It's important to beat test anxiety before it becomes a problem for more than testing.

> **Review Video:** <u>**Test Anxiety and Depression**</u>
> Visit mometrix.com/academy and enter code: 904704

Study Strategy

Being prepared for the test is necessary to combat anxiety, but what does being prepared look like? You may study for hours on end and still not feel prepared. What you need is a strategy for test prep. The next few pages outline our recommended steps to help you plan out and conquer the challenge of preparation.

Step 1: Scope Out the Test

Learn everything you can about the format (multiple choice, essay, etc.) and what will be on the test. Gather any study materials, course outlines, or sample exams that may be available. Not only will this help you to prepare, but knowing what to expect can help to alleviate test anxiety.

Step 2: Map Out the Material

Look through the textbook or study guide and make note of how many chapters or sections it has. Then divide these over the time you have. For example, if a book has 15 chapters and you have five days to study, you need to cover three chapters each day. Even better, if you have the time, leave an extra day at the end for overall review after you have gone through the material in depth.

If time is limited, you may need to prioritize the material. Look through it and make note of which sections you think you already have a good grasp on, and which need review. While you are studying, skim quickly through the familiar sections and take more time on the challenging parts. Write out your plan so you don't get lost as you go. Having a written plan also helps you feel more in control of the study, so anxiety is less likely to arise from feeling overwhelmed at the amount to cover.

Step 3: Gather Your Tools

Decide what study method works best for you. Do you prefer to highlight in the book as you study and then go back over the highlighted portions? Or do you type out notes of the important information? Or is it helpful to make flashcards that you can carry with you? Assemble the pens, index cards, highlighters, post-it notes, and any other materials you may need so you won't be distracted by getting up to find things while you study.

If you're having a hard time retaining the information or organizing your notes, experiment with different methods. For example, try color-coding by subject with colored pens, highlighters, or post-it notes. If you learn better by hearing, try recording yourself reading your notes so you can listen while in the car, working out, or simply sitting at your desk. Ask a friend to quiz you from your flashcards, or try teaching someone the material to solidify it in your mind.

Step 4: Create Your Environment

It's important to avoid distractions while you study. This includes both the obvious distractions like visitors and the subtle distractions like an uncomfortable chair (or a too-comfortable couch that makes you want to fall asleep). Set up the best study environment possible: good lighting and a comfortable work area. If background music helps you focus, you may want to turn it on, but otherwise keep the room quiet. If you are using a computer to take notes, be sure you don't have any other windows open, especially applications like social media, games, or anything else that could distract you. Silence your phone and turn off notifications. Be sure to keep water close by so you stay hydrated while you study (but avoid unhealthy drinks and snacks).

Also, take into account the best time of day to study. Are you freshest first thing in the morning? Try to set aside some time then to work through the material. Is your mind clearer in the afternoon or evening? Schedule your study session then. Another method is to study at the same time of day that you will take the test, so that your brain gets used to working on the material at that time and will be ready to focus at test time.

Step 5: Study!

Once you have done all the study preparation, it's time to settle into the actual studying. Sit down, take a few moments to settle your mind so you can focus, and begin to follow your study plan. Don't give in to distractions or let yourself procrastinate. This is your time to prepare so you'll be ready to fearlessly approach the test. Make the most of the time and stay focused.

Of course, you don't want to burn out. If you study too long you may find that you're not retaining the information very well. Take regular study breaks. For example, taking five minutes out of every hour to walk briskly, breathing deeply and swinging your arms, can help your mind stay fresh.

As you get to the end of each chapter or section, it's a good idea to do a quick review. Remind yourself of what you learned and work on any difficult parts. When you feel that you've mastered the material, move on to the next part. At the end of your study session, briefly skim through your notes again.

But while review is helpful, cramming last minute is NOT. If at all possible, work ahead so that you won't need to fit all your study into the last day. Cramming overloads your brain with more information than it can process and retain, and your tired mind may struggle to recall even previously learned information when it is overwhelmed with last-minute study. Also, the urgent nature of cramming and the stress placed on your brain contribute to anxiety. You'll be more likely to go to the test feeling unprepared and having trouble thinking clearly.

So don't cram, and don't stay up late before the test, even just to review your notes at a leisurely pace. Your brain needs rest more than it needs to go over the information again. In fact, plan to finish your studies by noon or early afternoon the day before the test. Give your brain the rest of the day to relax or focus on other things, and get a good night's sleep. Then you will be fresh for the test and better able to recall what you've studied.

Step 6: Take a practice test

Many courses offer sample tests, either online or in the study materials. This is an excellent resource to check whether you have mastered the material, as well as to prepare for the test format and environment.

Check the test format ahead of time: the number of questions, the type (multiple choice, free response, etc.), and the time limit. Then create a plan for working through them. For example, if you have 30 minutes to take a 60-question test, your limit is 30 seconds per question. Spend less time on the questions you know well so that you can take more time on the difficult ones.

If you have time to take several practice tests, take the first one open book, with no time limit. Work through the questions at your own pace and make sure you fully understand them. Gradually work up to taking a test under test conditions: sit at a desk with all study materials put away and set a timer. Pace yourself to make sure you finish the test with time to spare and go back to check your answers if you have time.

After each test, check your answers. On the questions you missed, be sure you understand why you missed them. Did you misread the question (tests can use tricky wording)? Did you forget the information? Or was it something you hadn't learned? Go back and study any shaky areas that the practice tests reveal.

Taking these tests not only helps with your grade, but also aids in combating test anxiety. If you're already used to the test conditions, you're less likely to worry about it, and working through tests until you're scoring well gives you a confidence boost. Go through the practice tests until you feel comfortable, and then you can go into the test knowing that you're ready for it.

Test Tips

On test day, you should be confident, knowing that you've prepared well and are ready to answer the questions. But aside from preparation, there are several test day strategies you can employ to maximize your performance.

First, as stated before, get a good night's sleep the night before the test (and for several nights before that, if possible). Go into the test with a fresh, alert mind rather than staying up late to study.

Try not to change too much about your normal routine on the day of the test. It's important to eat a nutritious breakfast, but if you normally don't eat breakfast at all, consider eating just a protein bar. If you're a coffee drinker, go ahead and have your normal coffee. Just make sure you time it so that the caffeine doesn't wear off right in the middle of your test. Avoid sugary beverages, and drink enough water to stay hydrated but not so much that you need a restroom break 10 minutes into the test. If your test isn't first thing in the morning, consider going for a walk or doing a light workout before the test to get your blood flowing.

Allow yourself enough time to get ready, and leave for the test with plenty of time to spare so you won't have the anxiety of scrambling to arrive in time. Another reason to be early is to select a good seat. It's helpful to sit away from doors and windows, which can be distracting. Find a good seat, get out your supplies, and settle your mind before the test begins.

When the test begins, start by going over the instructions carefully, even if you already know what to expect. Make sure you avoid any careless mistakes by following the directions.

Then begin working through the questions, pacing yourself as you've practiced. If you're not sure on an answer, don't spend too much time on it, and don't let it shake your confidence. Either skip it and come back later, or eliminate as many wrong answers as possible and guess among the remaining ones. Don't dwell on these questions as you continue—put them out of your mind and focus on what lies ahead.

Be sure to read all of the answer choices, even if you're sure the first one is the right answer. Sometimes you'll find a better one if you keep reading. But don't second-guess yourself if you do immediately know the answer. Your gut instinct is usually right. Don't let test anxiety rob you of the information you know.

If you have time at the end of the test (and if the test format allows), go back and review your answers. Be cautious about changing any, since your first instinct tends to be correct, but make sure you didn't misread any of the questions or accidentally mark the wrong answer choice. Look over any you skipped and make an educated guess.

At the end, leave the test feeling confident. You've done your best, so don't waste time worrying about your performance or wishing you could change anything. Instead, celebrate the successful completion of this test. And finally, use this test to learn how to deal with anxiety even better next time.

> **Review Video:** 5 Tips to Beat Test Anxiety
> Visit mometrix.com/academy and enter code: 570656

Important Qualification

Not all anxiety is created equal. If your test anxiety is causing major issues in your life beyond the classroom or testing center, or if you are experiencing troubling physical symptoms related to your anxiety, it may be a sign of a serious physiological or psychological condition. If this sounds like your situation, we strongly encourage you to seek professional help.

Thank You

We at Mometrix would like to extend our heartfelt thanks to you, our friend and patron, for allowing us to play a part in your journey. It is a privilege to serve people from all walks of life who are unified in their commitment to building the best future they can for themselves.

The preparation you devote to these important testing milestones may be the most valuable educational opportunity you have for making a real difference in your life. We encourage you to put your heart into it—that feeling of succeeding, overcoming, and yes, conquering will be well worth the hours you've invested.

We want to hear your story, your struggles and your successes, and if you see any opportunities for us to improve our materials so we can help others even more effectively in the future, please share that with us as well. **The team at Mometrix would be absolutely thrilled to hear from you!** So please, send us an email (support@mometrix.com) and let's stay in touch.

If you'd like some additional help, check out these other resources we offer for your exam:

http://MometrixFlashcards.com/VIRGINIA

Additional Bonus Material

Due to our efforts to try to keep this book to a manageable length, we've created a link that will give you access to all of your additional bonus material.

Please visit http://www.mometrix.com/bonus948/virginiavcla to access the information.